Being Black in America's Schools

BEING BLACK
IN
AMERICA'S SCHOOLS

A Student-Educator-Reformer's Call for Change

BRIAN RASHAD FULLER

www.kensingtonbooks.com

DAFINA BOOKS are published by

Kensington Publishing Corp.
900 Third Ave.
New York, NY 10022

All Kensington Titles, Imprints, and Distributed Lines are available at special quantity discounts for bulk purchases for sales promotions, premiums, fund-raising, and educational or institutional use. Special book excerpts or customized printings can also be created to fit specific needs. For details, write or phone the office of the Kensington special sales manager: Kensington Publishing Corp, 900 Third Ave., New York, NY 10022, Attn: Special Sales Department, Phone: 1-800-221-2647.

The DAFINA logo is a trademark of Kensington Publishing Corp.

ISBN: 978-1-4967-4660-3

First Kensington Hardcover Edition: August 2024

ISBN-13: 978-1-4967-4662-7 (ebook)

10 9 8 7 6 5 4 3 2 1

Printed in the United States of America

Library of Congress Control Number: 2024934886

To Black children and any other child who has ever felt marginalized, I dedicate this book to you. This book is my love letter to you. I write these words as a declaration that you are enough just as you are and your experiences matter even when the world around you consistently says otherwise. When the world acts as if you are not important and attempts to erase you or diminish you, I want you to know that you are seen. My desire is that this book will inspire adults, who were once children just like you, to create an education system that empowers you, heals you, excites you, and ignites you to discover your phenomenal light within.

With love,
Brian Rashad Fuller

Contents

Foreword

OVER ONE HUNDRED AND FIFTY years ago, the path to freedom for approximately four million Black people meant traversing the wilderness on a perilous journey from Southern states to the Northeastern region of the United States. Many enslaved Black people attempted that journey, but few were successful. Harriet Tubman, my fourth great-aunt, defied those odds and made the journey not only for herself but for many enslaved people, inevitably bringing them to freedom. She made it her responsibility to ensure that every person with her completed their journey to the freedom-land. When thinking about her story, I revere her bravery, strength, and strategic mind to accomplish such feats. She knew, at her core, freedom was not only her birthright but was everyone else's. She believed that all people were created equal and knew a grave injustice was being committed through slavery and oppression. That belief propelled her to become the freedom fighter and abolitionist that we know her as today.

Freedom is an uphill battle and will hopefully not be a forever fight. I believe now more than ever that the pathway to freedom is found through education. Harriet had no formal education; as we know formal education was not afforded to enslaved people, but she understood the importance of learning and she used her knowledge to set herself and many others free. She used knowledge of the land, knowledge of self, and knowledge of faith to see her through. Harriet also understood that freedom was not only a physical condition but a mental one, advocating that those in bondage develop a freedom mindset in order to save themselves from the destructive slave mentality.

Similarly, public schools in this country have the opportunity to use knowledge to help free millions of young minds, yet instead, we keep them captive. We keep them captive through gross miseducation practices such as actively defunding schools; rezoning districts; banning, excluding, destroying vital African American history; and much more. Our battle for freedom has now evolved into a push for inclusive, honest, and liberatory education in our schools. However, in our current climate, we have much misinformation and political division that impedes this fight and hurts our children in the process. Learning in institutions that were not historically built for all of us, with materials that were not written by us, and with no control over the educational delivery, has created the conditions for false and harmful narratives to continue to be spread to young, impressionable minds. One recent example is how there was a push in Texas to rebrand slavery as "involuntary relocation."

Since the 1954 landmark ruling of *Brown v. Board of Education* to desegregate schools, our nation has been under the guise that our educational institutions have drastically improved for minorities across this country. Yet many of us who have experienced public schools in the years since the landmark ruling know firsthand that this notion does not hold true. Many of our nation's schools actually took decades to legally integrate after 1954, with many still segregated today. Aside from the racial segregation that happens today in our schools as a consequence of neighborhood redlining practices, there is also a more acceptable racialization that occurs in schools as a result of standardized testing and "tracked" classes. Millions of Black and Brown children experience an education that is separate and unequal from their peers all because of standardized tests, tests that were racist at their inception.

Like millions of other Black children in America, I experienced the consequences of an educational system dedicated to keeping us separate and unequal. And worse, while I was being separated from my Black and Brown peers for the sake of being deemed high-achieving, I was not being exposed to our true history as Black people in this country. As a result of narratives told that were out of our control, I, like millions of others, was experiencing an erasure of my culture, history, and personhood while in school. Historically our people have recognized the miseducation we receive; the Black Panthers created a ten-point program in 1966 that spoke to this, with the fifth point of the program stating, "We want education for our people that exposes the true nature of this decadent American society. We want education that teaches us our true history and our role in the present-day society." Though written fifty-eight years ago, their words are just as accurate today. We must take action, teach our true American history, and stop the deliberate miseducation that takes place in our schools daily. For a fair chance, our children desperately need to be freed.

With that said, I am committed to aligning myself with others who are on the mission of liberating our people like Harriet did not so many years ago. I strongly believe that Brian Fuller is one of those individuals, and this book will act as a beacon for the liberation process for our children. I deeply connect with Brian's educational journey as we share many similar stories of growing up in the American education system even though we grew up in different states. I know many other Americans will feel just as connected to this story as they read his words. Education is our pathway to freedom, and this book brilliantly uncovers the lived educational experience of Black and Brown Americans in our country—showcasing what keeps us captive while giving keen insights on what can free us. With a dynamic story told from the perspective of a young Black student in America as well as a Black educator, this book will shed light on the parts of our educational system and society that are often kept in the shadows.

Before her passing, Harriet famously stated, "I go to prepare a place for you." When I think about what Brian has written, I think of the preparation of an educational system that will empower our children. This book will impart valuable knowledge and open space to humanize an experience that is often ignored. Educational empowerment for Black and Brown children in this country is one of the major social justice issues of our time and is imperative for the betterment of our society and our world. This book needs to be read, discussed, and heeded. This book is what our time calls for—a story that will begin to create a pathway toward the liberation of America's children.

—*Abdul P. Tubman, MBA*

Blow Up the Center

THE CONUNDRUM OF "BLACK STUDENT achievement" has been an American obsession since the start of the compulsory national education project almost a century ago. If you Google the words "Black student achievement," you will come across these various headlines from articles, stories, and research studies spanning many decades: "Why Are Black Students Lagging?" (2002), "Do Black Males Need Special Schools?" (1991), "Black Student College Graduation Rates Remain Low" (2006), "A Different Kind of Education for Black Children" (2008), "Addressing the African American Achievement Gap" (2018), "Schools are Still Segregated, and Black Children are Paying a Price" (2020). And these few I've highlighted here are just the tip of the iceberg. What is happening specifically with Black students, and by extension all students who can recognize the experience of being outside the metaphorical center, all students who have been historically marginalized in our American educational system? These are the students, who by trying to navigate that system, experience most intimately its captivity. These are the students that the so-called "founding fathers" of our country could not have imagined were deserving of an education, students outside their dream of America, tainted by White supremacy.

How do we fix this problem? There have been talks, debates, books, studies, seminars, and research for decades attempting to address a pressing problem, yet still, the prevailing issue exists. I have read these headlines and seen these statistics over and over again. The constant rhetoric that suggests Black student achievement is somehow inadequate is suffocating. And candidly, the incessant litany of data and discussion on this issue, for me, as a Black man working in education, was exhausting. Already after five years, I was disillusioned and looking for a lifeline. Then, in 2018, I heard a powerful story from an informed voice that helped shed new insights on the pervasive challenge of the public narrative specifically around Black students, a story that illustrated for me how the power of narrative can inspire us to act toward a solution that will incite change in the system.

I was sitting in a room with a few of my colleagues from the New York City Department of Education, feeling slightly intimidated and excited. There were at least one hundred other brilliant educators from all parts of the country in this room. We were about to separate into smaller discussion groups to share personal insights from what we had just learned during this workshop. I looked around, and it seemed like I was one of the youngest people present. The title of the seminar was "One Structure at a Time: Dismantling Systemic Racism in Institutions." This workshop was one of many I had attended during my time at the five-day long Summit for Courageous Conversation in Philadelphia hosted by Glenn Singleton's Pacific Education Group. The annual summit brought together educators, activists, and community leaders to learn how to achieve racial equity in education.

I had spent the earlier portion of the day listening to world-renowned social justice teachers, advocates, researchers, authors, and speakers. I was thrilled with the information I received. The words and teachings of so many dynamic individuals moved me deeply. Being in this workshop, I had the opportunity to share my perspective, but truthfully, I only wanted to soak up the knowledge like a sponge. We moved into our discussion groups for roughly thirty minutes and reflected on how we could use our roles to help dismantle systemic racism in our respective institutions. The conversations were rich. I enjoyed hearing various educators talk about what they had done and what they planned on doing with the information we learned during the conference.

After the breakouts, we came back together as a whole group to share with everyone in the room. The facilitators told us they would "open the floor" for anyone to share thoughts and highlights they had from their conversations. A few people spoke and expressed insights I thought were helpful. But nothing said was uniquely memorable until an older Black woman, probably in her mid-sixties, began to talk. I had noticed this woman before because she reminded me of Clair Huxtable from *The Cosby Show* and my grandmother. She had a regal authority about her that was evident. She was familiar and comforting to me as I've experienced a lot of older Black women who possess her same demeanor. Her voice was powerful, assured, caring, and filled with wisdom. As she began to speak, the room went silent.

She started out by telling a story about a newspaper article she read as a first-year teacher in Philadelphia. The article's headline stated that Black boys had the lowest graduation rates in the city, and the school board needed to take drastic measures to address the crisis. She went on to say that the newspaper article "ignited a fire" in her, and she knew she was in the right profession because she wanted to help "[her] people," young Black students in the city, to reach their full potential. The woman said she dedicated her career to "changing the headline." She continued by saying that in this year, 2018, only a few weeks before attending the summit, she had seen another newspaper article stating that Black boys had the lowest graduation rate in the city of Philadelphia. The headline continued to say it was a "crisis" that desperately needed to be addressed. Then her voice projected anger. "Why are we still seeing the same headlines after forty years?" she exclaimed. The woman went on to say that she believed she had spent a well-intentioned career merely "tinkering around the edges" of the problem. I could totally relate to her frustrations. She iterated how the educational initiatives and reforms over the years were only "quick fixes" but did not address the root of the problem.

She chuckled and then said that in her "old age she had become more radical," and now realized that we needed to stop just "tinkering around the edges" trying to change the education system. The time had come for us to go and "blow up the center" and start anew. She reminded us again that her career as an educator would be ending soon, but she hoped the younger folks in the room would spend their careers trying to "blow up the center" instead of "tinkering around the edges." Her words inspired us, and the crowd reacted with snaps and verbal agreement. As the room erupted in response to this seasoned educator's powerful narrative, I began to contemplate how systemic racism is the symbolic center in our education system and what it would mean to truly dismantle it.

Three years later, in 2021, I found myself reflecting on all of the disheartening events that had transpired the previous year—the murders of George Floyd, Ahmaud Arbery, and Breonna Taylor, to name a few, and of course the COVID-19 pandemic that had completely disrupted the world as we knew it. As I watched hundreds of thousands of people across the country call for governments to rethink the inherently racist structures within our society, most notably the criminal justice system, I couldn't help but remember the soul-stirring words that my elder had said at the summit I had attended a few years back and the inadequate state of our education system. I asked myself, what has brought us to this place? Why do we keep reliving the same experiences year after year? I believe that as a society we have quickly come to the grim realization that the criminal justice system in our country is racist to the core and needs to be dismantled. But why have we not said the same about our American public education system? Do we not want an educational system that unifies us all, instead of one that in many ways upholds the ideals that perpetuate systemic racism?

So, to honor the woman's brilliant words and my journey as a Black male in America, I am sharing my story of navigating the world and the American public education system. I am sharing an American story that I honestly believe is begging to be told. And throughout this book, I will illustrate a harrowing truth about our American education system, which is that our public schools are responsible for the largest, most coherent waging of psychological warfare in this nation. I will uncover elements of the system that I believe are inherently racist, destructive, and psychologically damaging not only to Black children but all students that are outside of this symbolic center.

If there is any one thing that most Americans can agree on at this moment, it may be that we are living in polarizing times. What's more, we are inundated with data, statistics, facts, hot takes, misinformation, tweets, TED Talks, and more while we attempt to explain our world's most pressing issues or shape the ideas that will create the future. This book flows from a deep commitment of mine to storytelling, to a belief in the way personal stories humanize the policies and systems that give rise to present inequities. This conviction is why I decided to balance autobiography with analysis, to use both my own story and my expertise to shed light specifically on the inequities that are faced in America's school systems. The three sections of this book track the educational life cycle of most Americans, starting from primary school moving to secondary school and ending with college or career, as seen through my eyes.

As a lifelong educator and student, I believe what we most deeply need in this climate is more understanding of one another, and powerful storytelling that will inspire us to action. Only a story can cut through the noise. I hope to use the power of storytelling to begin the process of "blowing up the center" of the American education system as we know it. Isn't it time to challenge the system to actually hold true to America's promise? If not now, then when?

Being Black in America's Schools

PART I

Early and Primary Education

CHAPTER 1

Lil' Man

... to handicap a [child] by teaching him that his black face is a curse and that his struggle to change his condition is hopeless is the worst sort of lynching. It kills one's aspirations....
—CARTER G. WOODSON, *THE MIS-EDUCATION OF THE NEGRO*, 1933

WHEN WE ARRIVED IN THE visitation room at Chesterfield County Jail, my father was already sitting behind a thick glass partition next to a phone. He smiled at us, but he seemed ashamed. My grandmother picked up the phone first and started to talk to her son. Then my mother spoke with my father briefly. I wasn't paying attention to what was said, but I noticed closely how they each glanced at me with some despair in their eyes. I could only imagine the shame and embarrassment my parents must have felt bringing their child into an environment like this, a place that, unknown to us then, we would experience together for decades to come.

I was completely numb. Crying was not an option, so I stood there, internalizing my feelings, emotions that my three-year-old mind could barely handle. I felt like I needed to explode. I wanted to scream or run out of the building. Instead, I froze. I was still and quiet, not knowing what to do. While I stood in silence, I witnessed my father, mother, and grandmother participating in the same behavior. They all were internalizing their emotions, attempting to make the most out of the situation—a ritual they mastered through a lifetime as Black people in America. This would be the first of the many times I would see them deal with life this way and I learned to mimic this behavior.

As I stood there, my eyes wandered around. I looked at the glass partitions next to me, and I realized that all the other men behind the glass looked like me. There were other Black men in this jail. I saw their faces, and their faces stuck with me. My racialized sense of self, at this point, had already been developed. I was aware that I was Black, and seeing not only my father, a Black man, but many other Black men behind those glass partitions left a deep imprint on my mind. If my father had done something bad to be placed in jail, did it mean that all these other Black men who looked like me had done something bad as well? Could I also do something wrong to be put in this place? At the time, I had no idea how mass incarceration in America plagued the Black community. I wasn't then aware of this statistic: one in four Black children in America will experience having an incarcerated parent during their childhood. All I knew was every man I saw in this jail was a reflection of myself. My sense of shame, fear, and confusion started to rise. I was heartbroken that I couldn't hug my father or sit on his lap and I felt confused because the person I thought was a bigger version of me was now in jail and could no longer protect me.

My grandmother looked at me and motioned for me to come over to the window. As I walked up to the glass and my mother picked me up so I could reach the phone, I could not explain how I felt. My stomach hurt, I felt exhausted and weak all in the same moment—physical symptoms of the psychological blow I was experiencing. My hero was behind this thick glass, trapped and powerless. Why did this happen to us? To me?

As I SIT here today, an education leader and a concerned American putting words to my story for the first time, a burning question comes to mind: What does a child learn about themselves before entering school? I believe this question, while simple, is one of the most important inquiries our society should make when considering the structural design of an education system and the effects that system will have on a child and how it responds to what is actually happening in the wide range of American families. Many scholars before me have connected racialized early childhood experiences in our country to the distorted self-development of children in America.

As I began to understand my own early childhood experiences, it became clear to me just how our racialized society shaped my mind before I even set foot into a school building. Research shows that before the age of five, at least 85 percent of a child's mental development has already taken place, and this development will significantly impact them for the rest of their lives. And if it is clear in my story, it made me wonder, how many children are being impacted by these early childhood experiences in this country—especially Black children like myself, and all others at the margins?

In 1995, Dr. Vincent J. Feletti, in collaboration with Dr. Robert Anda of the Centers for Disease Control and Prevention (CDC), began an influential study on adverse childhood experiences (ACEs) and how they affect adult health outcomes. According to the CDC, an ACE is defined as a potentially traumatic experience in childhood. They are usually organized into three categories: abuse, neglect, and household challenges such as experiencing an incarcerated household member, as I did. The fact that Black and Latino children experience an incarcerated household member at a higher rate than White children is well-documented but also, according to the nonprofit and nonpartisan child research center Child Trends, 61 percent of Black American children who are not also Latino and 51 percent of Latino children have lived through at least one ACE as compared to 40 percent of their White American counterparts. Further, stress from ACEs has been proven to build up over time and negatively impact adolescent and adult educational outcomes. Chief Clinical Officer at Starr Commonwealth, the renowned clinical psychologist and author Dr. Caelan Soma states, "All kids, especially in this day and age, experience extreme stress from time to time. It is more common than we think." I would go further. I believe that all Black children, and all of those who have been traditionally marginalized by the education system, experience this extreme stress inherently just by being born and living in an American society shaped by a White supremacist caste system.

———————

I REMEMBER THE sterile, cold feeling of the air in the visitation room. I leaned forward out of my mother's arms and reached out my small hand to touch the glass. My father touched the other side with his much larger hand and my mother looked at us both with tears in her eyes. I don't remember what was said, but I do recall how I felt. I was hurt. It hurt me deeply that my father, someone who I thought the world of, was now a person locked up in jail. I was his Lil' Man, and I felt abandoned by him and confused about the world I now lived in. My hand on that glass was the closest I could get to him, and a part of me knew that my life would forever be different because of this encounter. My reality as I knew it shifted and my sense of safety changed. I would come to realize later that this moment birthed a deep sense of uncertainty in my world that would take years for me to shake. What was possible in a society where my family and I could experience so much pain?

With my hand still on the glass, I looked at my father and he told me he loved me. I said, "I love you, too." After that, it was time for us to go. My mother and grandmother each took one of my hands, and we left without anyone saying a word.

———————

"COME HERE, LIL' MAN. Come dance with me!" Aunt Charnelle shouted to me from my grandparents' apartment patio. It was July of 1993, eight months before my father's arrest. For the first two and a half years of my life, my father was in the army. His assignment was in Fort Campbell, Kentucky, interrupted by a remote tour in Somalia for the US peace intervention, Operation Restore Hope, while my mother, Sheryl, and I held down the home front in South Carolina. We occasionally saw him or spoke with him on the phone but this Fourth of July weekend he was back from deployment and the amount of face-to-face time I had with him was not the norm. I loved every bit of it.

I darted excitedly through the yard behind my idol—my father. Alcohol was flowing, meats were grilling, Mary J. Blige's classic hit "Real Love" from her debut album *What's the 411?* blasted from the stereo while my two aunts, my father's older sisters, danced freely on the patio. Brian, my father and namesake, and his younger brother, my uncle Patrick, eagerly shot video footage of everything about that day, images I would watch years later with bittersweet nostalgia.

"Come here, Lil' Man!" was a common catchphrase in my family. Lil' Man or Lil' Brian was what everyone called me, and the big man, "Big Brian," was my father. I bore a strong resemblance to Big Brian in both looks and mannerisms. "You look just like your daddy! He could've spit you out himself, boy" were words I consistently heard in my early years. At this point in my life, I had only been described in association with him. My existence was interconnected completely with this six-foot-tall, lean, handsome, and charismatic Black man. In my mind, I was simply a smaller version of him, and he, a bigger version of me. Our intertwined identities gave me a sense of security.

Though I didn't know it then, not all was ideal. My parents were beginning to realize the challenges of navigating society as young adults who, without educational credentials above high school, were struggling to grab their piece of the "American dream." Their world was changing fast, and they were failing to keep up with the pace.

But today the music was still playing, now the Isley Brothers. "Come dance with Daddy," he said to me lovingly as he started doing the classic "'90s bop" that many hip-hop artists did in their music videos at the time (think Kris Kross in "Jump"). I immediately began to mimic his dance moves, while my aunts cheered me on from the sidelines, "Go 'head Lil' Man, go 'head, Lil' B!"

It gives me solace to know that as I was forming my definition of self I was also shaped by experiences of love, joy, and music. But this is what made the grief of losing my father to incarceration that much more devastating.

———

BLACK YOUTHS' EARLY childhood trauma tied to the negative racialized experiences of their parents is as American as Friday night football. History has proven this. One story in particular I have inexplicably felt connected to is that of James Van Evers, son of civil rights activist Medgar Evers. James was only three years old when his father was brutally murdered in his driveway in front of him and the rest of his siblings. When I learned of his story early in my childhood, I always wondered how he felt when this happened and what impact this heinous act had on him. Though my father was not physically murdered when I saw him in the jailhouse for the first time at the age of three, reflecting back candidly, it felt like a death to me. Now as an adult, I understand the sociological implications of what I was feeling. What I was witnessing was the manifestation of a "social death."

Social death, a term coined by sociologists Orlando Patterson and Zygmunt Bauman and used by historians of slavery and the Holocaust, is defined as the condition of people not being accepted as fully human by their wider society. The moment my father became an inmate behind the glass partition I knew he was socially dead. What's even more agonizing now is I understand the grief I was truly experiencing was the realization that he was socially dead before he was ever brought to the jailhouse. Seeing the other Black men there with him made me understand we were all socially dead. Sadly, I was not only grieving my father but also myself.

Like me, Black children and other children at the margins of our society have been grieving their deaths along with their parents' deaths since the inception of this country. Author and professor Dr. Sheila Flemming-Hunter writes of how the newly emancipated Black children of enslaved people at the end of the Civil War "had witnessed the violence, injustice, and denial of individual freedom perpetrated on their mothers and fathers" which remains an ever-present dynamic in Black American life. The history of Black children witnessing the violence our society wages on their caretakers is the basis of their early childhood trauma and shapes for us what it means to be American. That trauma is inescapable, and that trauma is what develops the identity of Black children and many other children before they ever enter school.

I WAS BORN on March 1, 1991, in South Carolina, two days before Rodney King, an unarmed Black man, was brutally beaten by four police officers on an interstate in Los Angeles. On March 7, three days after my mother and I returned home from the hospital, the video footage of the beating was released to the American public. My mother recalls watching that video with her siblings at my grandparents' home while I was only a few days old. She felt sick to her stomach. There she was, a young mother only a few days after giving birth to her only Black son, watching one of the most brutal public beatings of a Black man by police she had ever seen. She was terrified and she desperately wanted to do whatever she could to protect me from having any experience similar to Mr. King's. Accordingly, my Black American family life, from my first week on earth, occurred against the backdrop of safety and protection from the violence of White supremacy.

Black Americans have historically had a justified distrust for many institutions in American society, institutions that, like the police, are rooted in the violent experience of White supremacy. For example, one can start with de jure segregation, redlining practices, the CDC's unethical mistreatment of Black syphilis patients in the Tuskegee Study, or the FBI's belligerent surveillance and harassment of Dr. Martin Luther King Jr. through COINTELPRO to understand the legitimate precedent for these misgivings. The American education system is not exempt from this long cycle of harm and distrust. From the vicious desegregation of our nation's schools to the post-desegregation tradition of cruelty toward marginalized people upon entry into the education system, the apprehension many Black people have toward public education is well-established and, in many cases, well-founded. The challenge of navigating a broken education system is one many Black people have accepted as an American reality.

I learned of this legacy in my own family early on. My mother had me at the tender age of nineteen and was determined to be a good parent. She was the first in her family to go to college. This was a big accomplishment for her, and at the time, my grandparents were thrilled at the thought of all the possibilities in her future. She was a part of the American trend during the late 1980s and early 1990s when Black enrollment in colleges and universities reached record highs. My mother enrolled at South Carolina State University, a well-known HBCU. Black women accounted for a majority of this increase, and it continued throughout the decade, increasing Black presence in higher education over 30 percent by the end of the 1990s. Many of my family members, and many scholars, attribute this statistic to the impact of shows like *The Cosby Show* and *A Different World* on the American public in the late 1980s.

I was my parents' only child together and the first grandchild on both sides of the family. My grandparents had high hopes for my mother and when she became pregnant, they were extremely disappointed. They, as Black baby boomers who had grown up in Jim Crow South Carolina, understood the gravity of what it meant to have their daughter attend college—an accomplishment neither of them had attained. They knew that her life would drastically change after having a baby. And initially, they were not supportive of the pregnancy. Despite this, my mother insisted on having me, a decision she made sure I knew was the best one of her life each time she would sing her favorite Lauryn Hill song, "To Zion," changing the words to say, "To Brian." Once my mother realized she was pregnant, she made the difficult choice to drop out of college. Her choice is not uncommon within the Black community. According to recent data, Black students finish college at a much lower rate than all other races and ethnicities in this country—only 45.9 percent graduate. This is partly related to the stat that over 65 percent of all Black college students are pursuing their degree independently, meaning they are balancing work and home responsibilities. For my mother, the responsibility of now having a child meant she had to leave the university and move back in with my grandparents and her younger siblings. My mother's deferred dreams would become the contaminated oxygen in the atmosphere of my early childhood.

IF MY MOTHER'S deferred dreams gave me breath, however imperfectly, my father's deadened ambitions became the toxic water that I ingested. My father had just turned twenty when my mother became pregnant. Immediately after hearing the news, he decided to enlist in the army—leaving behind any possibility of continuing his formal education. Enlisting in the army seemed like the best option for him, as it has for many other Black and Brown men in his position. As a result, in March of 1991, my father was in basic training when I was born.

He was deployed to Somalia in 1993. His time there deeply impacted him, he would later explain to me. He felt lied to and tricked going there on a "peace intervention" where he, as a Black American man, was not welcomed by fellow Black men and women from Somalia as much as he expected to be. Additionally, the repetitive death and violence he witnessed was traumatizing for him and would lead him to be diagnosed with PTSD years later. Coming back from Somalia, my father was confused and had lost a complete sense of who he was and what he wanted out of life. At the time, he did not articulate his thoughts or feelings, so his choice not to reenlist was a surprise to my twenty-one-year-old mother. The choice made her incredibly upset. She was concerned about our well-being and my father's ability to financially provide for the family. Unbeknownst to my mother at the time, my father shared her same concerns.

After enough inquiry through various stages of my life, I have learned that my father had a "fairly pleasant" school experience until he moved to "the country" or Dalzell, South Carolina—a small, rural community close to Sumter. When they settled there, my father and his siblings were bullied by many Black kids and some of the Black teachers at their new school because of how they spoke and dressed. This led them to get into several fights with other students. My father felt that many of his peers, teachers, and even the principal disliked him because they thought he was, in his words, an "uppity nigga." My father even had a physical altercation with the principal, leading the school to suspend him multiple times and even threaten expulsion.

One of the tragic consequences of White supremacy is the notion that Black people are not inherently as smart as their White counterparts, a lie that has historically been accepted to some degree by the majority of Americans and sometimes internalized by Black people. During my childhood, my grandmother spoke passionately about how she often advocated for my aunts and uncles to not be placed in remedial courses. My aunts and uncles would often express how their middle and high school teachers would tell them that "they were not going to be successful in life" or "would be lucky if they graduated" or unfairly punish them. What my father was experiencing when he was bullied because of the way he spoke and performed in school was similar to what I would experience some years later.

I often wonder how my father's early childhood experiences were linked to his eventual incarceration. My father was bullied before he even went to school. My grandmother would often tell stories of how my father refused to play outside with other kids because he just wanted to be near her and feared bullying from those children. Each time my grandmother would have to leave him he would become hysterical; he even ran behind moving cars she was in, pleading for her to return.

As a young Black mother, my grandmother knew that the world she lived in was harsh and believed she needed to toughen her son up to protect him from the dangers of a White supremacist reality. There was no room in the world for vulnerability or sensitivity and as his mother, she needed to ensure her son could survive. When my father would come home scared, after being bullied by the neighborhood kids, she would make him go back out to fight them or "there would be consequences at home." She would also lock him outside the house sometimes in efforts to make him play with other kids and separate himself from her. These tactics, she said, were out of love because she knew she would not always be there to protect her son and wanted to make sure that he could look out for himself. She was a strong Black woman and her son needed to be a strong Black man.

These harsh realities and harsh responses have spanned generations. All of these similarly disheartening stories my family shared with me taught me about the uniquely racialized experience of American schools. Early on I knew that life was different being Black in America, therefore life would be different being Black in America's schools. I knew this before I could even verbalize it. I knew this way before I ever entered a school building.

CHILDREN, FROM A developmental standpoint, essentially experience an entire life before the age of five. It is truly remarkable what happens in a child's brain even within their first three years. Because of this, I strongly urge educators, policymakers, and all those interested in the structure of our American educational system to acknowledge and understand that those early life experiences play a critical role in how we educate our children. This system will only be effective if we include the lived realities of all of America's children—most importantly those too often ignored. There are elements of my early childhood story that may seem uniquely mine, but they are not. My story is an American one—it's just the American story that's been buried.

Visiting my father in jail quickly made me understand what it meant to be a child on the margins of society. I was one of approximately 990,000 Black children in America who experienced a parent incarcerated in 1994. Though that number was large, America's prison population has grown immensely since then. In 2022, a minimum of 2.5 million Black children experienced a parent who was incarcerated.

I can't help but wonder: Can any of those other 990,000 Black children recount a story similar to mine? Or how many of those 990,000 are parents of the 2.5 million today? And, most importantly, what role did school play in their lives before or after this experience?

The numbers, though staggering, only scratch the surface. They only grow when one incorporates other minority groups into the mix who are also incarcerated at higher rates than their White counterparts. Studies show that parental incarceration significantly increases poor student outcomes for those students in our public schools. But even if a child hasn't looked in the eyes of their incarcerated parent or seen a sea of Black faces locked up behind bars as I did, I am certain there are many other negative racialized events that have shaped the outlook of their world, from police violence to inadequate housing to poverty to daily discrimination. Research suggests that early childhood racial stress trauma (RST) is severely underreported in this country and has devastating consequences.

So what are we doing as a society to address this trauma in our children? This is the question that keeps me up at night. And further, how are we altering the way we think about education based on these uniquely differentiated American experiences? We must confront the large number of children in this country who have childless childhoods, whose coming-of-age stories are full of racialized, social trauma at the hands of structural racism. Their childhoods have been brutally stripped from them the moment they are born and if we do not reimagine an education system that fully addresses that terror—that spiritual and mental warfare that being born in America causes—then the only question I have is what is the point of having an education system at all?

CHAPTER 2

A Terrible Weight

*Children, not yet aware that it is dangerous to look too
deeply at anything, look at everything... and draw their
own conclusions.... [A] Black child, looking at the world
around him, though he cannot know quite what to make of
it, is aware that there is a reason why his mother works so
hard, why his father is always on edge.... He is aware that
there is some terrible weight on his parents' shoulders
which menaces him. And it isn't long—in fact, it begins
when he is in school—before he discovers the shape of his
oppression.*
— JAMES BALDWIN, "A TALK TO TEACHERS," 1963

ON THE AFTERNOON OF MAY 23, 1951, three Black men entered
Pennsylvania Station in New York City and boarded the Pal-
metto, embarking on an eighteen-hour train journey down the
East Coast of the United States. The overnighter deposited them
on the platform in Charleston, South Carolina, at eight the next
morning. On that same morning, my grandmother Clara turned
three years old in her small home on sharecropper land in nearby
Clarendon County, South Carolina, where Dr. Kenneth Clark, one
of the three men, was headed. The psychology scholar had traveled

to South Carolina with top NAACP Legal Defense Fund lawyers and civil rights activists Thurgood Marshall and Robert Carter to re-create the famed doll test experiments he and his wife had designed and conducted from 1939 to 1940. In the original experiments, Black children, ages three to seven, were asked to look at black and white dolls and choose which one they preferred. A majority of the children, over 70 percent, showed a preference for the white doll, a result which Clark argued illustrated that these Black children were showcasing an internalized inferiority to their White counterparts. When the experiment was performed again in South Carolina, the results confirmed Clark's conclusions.

Thurgood Marshall planned to use the findings from Clarendon County as the basis for the argument that segregated schools in America were psychologically damaging to Black children and socially harmful to White children. His argument resulted in the historic 1954 *Brown v. Board of Education* decision to desegregate schools in the United States.

It's not lost on me that my grandmother and grandfather could have been in Clark's experiment. They were both living in Clarendon County and in the age range of tested children. It's possible they knew the children who were involved. I wonder if my grandparents had participated in the study, which doll would they have selected? Did they feel, even at that young age, they were inferior? They both attended segregated schools in South Carolina during their childhood and were raised in racist, segregated communities. What impact did this upbringing have on them psychologically? And how did their psyche impact my mother and later impact me? Would I have preferred a white doll over a black one at the age of three? Perhaps after my visit with my father in the jailhouse, I would have. And further, what role did my early classrooms play in perpetuating what I had already internalized about myself and my race by the time I was three? Has the desegregation of schools changed the result of the famed doll tests? Findings as recent as 2020 show that they have not. And when I begin to reflect on my school experience and the experiences of other Black and marginalized children, I understand why so much has gone unchanged in the past seventy years.

SEPTEMBER 3, 1994

"I just got my student loan money! Grab Lil' Man. We're going shopping!" my aunt Caprice said excitedly to my mother. My parents and I were back in Richmond, Virginia, living with my grandparents, my aunts, and my uncle. My mother was on a mission: find work and put me in the best preschool. And if I was going to be at the best preschool, I needed top-tier, brand-name clothes to match. My aunt knew my parents' financial circumstances, so she decided to use the money she recently received from her student loans to buy my wardrobe. There was no way her "Lil' Man" would not be the best-dressed in the room. So, with a small fraction of that money in tow, we went and bought some of the most stylish clothes a three-year-old could wear.

Both of my parents wanted to show the naysayers that their son would have the most sought-after opportunities available. After countless weeks of searching, my mother found a preschool she thought would be excellent. The only problem was that it was a private preschool where elite families paid a steep price to enroll their children—twelve thousand dollars a year. Both she and my father had not found work yet, so there was no way they could afford it. However, my mother knew the school was the place for me. She had always aspired to be a teacher, so she applied for a support staff role at the center, interviewed, and was hired to work with the younger children in the one-year-old classroom. And, as an employee, she was able to enroll her child there for a minimal fee of ten dollars per paycheck. As a result, in the fall of 1994, I was admitted into the three-year-old classroom at Children's Place in Chesterfield, Virginia.

Children's Place was a highly sought-after educational center in the Chesterfield-Richmond area. The affluent White community flocked to the school's approach to learning that was grounded in child-centered, Reggio Emilia-like philosophy. The center allowed children to learn purely through exploration of their individual interests. I was the only Black child in my classroom of ten and was one of three Black children out of the fifty or so students at Children's Place.

I entered the school, still processing the last few months of my life and their adverse circumstances. My father had only recently been released from jail, and I was uncertain if he could go back. Weeks before, we had moved back to Richmond from Sumter. I was quickly trying to make sense of the changes happening in my world and attempting to comprehend the societal experience of people who looked like my father and me. *Is jail normal for Black boys?* I carried these questions in my mind as I entered the preschool space.

Today, early childhood education is the best chance in our learning system to directly interrupt the legacy of racial trauma in the United States. Schools cannot prevent adverse childhood experiences, but they can and should help students to cope with them. On a positive note, in the past decade, as the research on early childhood trauma has become more mainstream, there has been a growing push for trauma-informed early childhood education, an approach that has been recently recommended by the US Department of Health and Human Services "as one method for promoting the socioemotional health of young children." However, all too often early childhood education is trivialized by our society as simply babysitting. It is consistently underfunded, under-prioritized, and under-professionalized when it should be the critical foundation of the American educational system. My early childhood education never reflected the world I was experiencing; it was not designed to acknowledge the trauma I had experienced as a Black child witnessing my Black father incarcerated.

Like many preschool students, I have fond memories of my early learning environment. My daily activities filled me with excitement, play, and laughter. My teachers were genuinely nice to me. Ms. Sherry was my favorite. She would give me an enormous

hug every time she saw me. I made friends with many of my classmates, and it was also comforting to have my mother in the
classroom next door. She made sure I was always treated well by
teachers and other staff members.

Despite these mostly positive experiences and my mother's fer-
vent advocacy, I always felt a strange sense of otherness at
Children's Place. This feeling, I believe now, did not come from any
treatment I received from my teachers or classmates but rather
from the challenge of processing the world of White supremacy.
My new friends in the preschool were all White and were all from
wealthy families. From what I understood, even at that young age,
my classmates' families were different from mine. After all, their
fathers had not been in jail to my knowledge, and their mothers
did not work at our school. Also, they spoke openly about their
families in a way that I did not. My mother always said, "Keep our
business our business. Don't talk to the other kids about our business." At home, my mother talked with my aunts about "the rich
parents," and I noticed she did not speak about us in the same way.
Many of the parents were lawyers, doctors, military generals, or
the like. As a three-year-old, I did not fully comprehend our financial circumstances, but I knew for sure we were not rich, and I
figured rich people did not go to jail.

Since the Obama era, funding for preschool education or rather
Head Start and Early Head Start programs has become a hot topic
in the public discourse. Many educators and policymakers alike
argue for universal preschool programs across the country, citing
the data that indicates better educational and career outcomes for
those children who have earlier access to school. Universal preschool has been promoted specifically to help support lower
income families and communities of color. The data is clear. What
is also clear is that these programs are expensive for our government, and many argue that although access to early childhood
education has proven benefits it is not a cost-effective investment
and that it is the American family that should be most responsible
for preparing their children for life success. As of December 2023,
only three states provide universal preschool programs for all four-

year-olds, but many cities and states across the country are in the process of allocating more resources into early childhood programs. This is an ongoing fight.

Though this fight for universal access to early education programs will be a long one, I do believe it is critically necessary. We need all children, especially those Black and historically marginalized children, to have access to early education to counter the harm our American society inflicts on them from birth. Going further, I believe emphatically that none of these programs will matter unless they become *high-quality* early childhood programs that resist the harms of racism, build self-efficacy, and promote a positive sense of self. I find it interesting that even in New York City, which has the most extensive pre-K system in America—enough free seats available for every four-year-old resident—many parents still pay, on average, sixteen thousand dollars for private preschools. Notably, the NYC private preschool market is one of the most competitive and most expensive in the country. Though pre-K is free and universal in the city, more affluent families still opt to pay a steep price to ensure quality early childhood learning opportunities. Like my mother, these parents understand the importance of early education. But, unlike my mother and many other Black parents, wealthy parents in New York City have the resources to pursue the best opportunities for their children.

In contrast, oftentimes Black and other traditionally marginalized families in America are structurally excluded from all early learning opportunities for their children because of a lack of resources. As a society we have begun to recognize this reality and are attempting to address it. This is substantial progress in the right direction. Still, even if we manage to develop widespread pre-K infrastructure, but neglect quality and fail to be intentional about the sociological role of these spaces, we risk more harm. In fact, in that case, we might be better off without them.

What is not being discussed enough, in my opinion, is the intentional countering of racial trauma that these early childhood learning centers have the opportunity to do and should be driving, public and private. Even in my own story, I had access to the most prestigious early childhood educational opportunity, but that private program still severely lacked what I needed as a Black child in America. As I continue to reflect on my early years in education, I can clearly see why the need for trauma-informed, liberatory pre-K is extremely important.

Feelings of separateness and alienation were my experience at Children's Place, but I hid those feelings as much as possible. Now I believe this repression was the start of convincing myself that validation in school from my teachers was more important than my own emotions. I felt good there, things were calm, and people were friendly. This is what I was beginning to learn that school was like—a place full of lovely White people with money who did not need to know that sometimes Black boys' fathers go to jail. Environments like this one started to feel safe for me, providing me the sense of consistency I had lost in the jail visitation room. It was a sense of security I would continue to long for and cling to throughout my childhood—a protection that, as I got older, I learned came at a high cost.

––––––––––

RESEARCH SHOWS THAT Black children in predominantly White spaces endure significant negative psychological consequences. Feelings of isolation and exclusion are common among Black students and other marginalized groups in predominantly White spaces. Further, these Black students often report more frequent experiences of racism and negative racialized behaviors directed toward them. There has been some debate, especially since *Brown v. Board of Education* (1954), that called for the re-separation of schools because of the known damage that White majority spaces can cause for minority students. Black thought leaders such as Malcolm X and others have questioned the true outcome of integration on the Black psyche. In a 1963 speech, Malcolm stated "we want separation, not segregation," meaning the right to educate ourselves instead of an education both socially and academically being forced upon Black people and other marginalized groups. In 2019, when I was facilitating a parent focus group for the NYC Department of

Education on a school integration plan in the Gowanus neighborhood of Brooklyn, Black and Latino parents consistently raised concerns about what negative impact the integration would have on their children. One mother in particular said to me in the circle of community members, "I do not want my child hurt by going to this mostly White school. The teachers may not understand him. The students might make him feel isolated. I worry about his safety."

I now understand the psychological toll learning in a predominantly White space had on me as a three- and four-year-old, a burden I continued to carry throughout my educational experience. As I write this, I want to be crystal clear. I am not saying that the White children or White teachers in those all-White spaces I learned in were acting with intentional malice. Actually, in my case, I am convinced it was quite the opposite. However, the psychological damage, as research shows, happens inherently when a child is "othered" in a space that is steeped in White supremacist values and ways of being. For Black children who insist on expressing their authentic selves, the system often punishes them directly and the damages of overly harsh discipline, disparate suspensions, and more are clear. But, just as damaging, if not more so, is the psychological impact of repression. There was not a space for my authentic self to show up in my pre-K and therefore I compartmentalized it, tucked it away. My response, I believe, is similar to the one many marginalized children have every day in America's schools. Either way, students who externalize or students who internalize their true selves misaligned with America's heritage of Whiteness in schools face dire consequences.

———

WHEN I WAS four, my mother made the sudden decision to leave my father, who was struggling to find employment and often absent. We moved back to Sumter, South Carolina, to live permanently with her parents. My experiences in kindergarten and first grade there were my first indication of the real and physical damages inflicted on students who are misaligned with the expectations and values of Whiteness in the classroom.

"Ms. Reed, Eric is looking at Brittany's paper," I said loudly to my first-grade teacher.

"No, I'm not. Shut up before I punch you in the face," Eric retorted, glaring at me.

My teacher then interjected, "Eric, get up and go to the back of the room now!"

"Thank you, Brian, for letting me know," she said as I felt validated.

By this point in the school year, my classmate Eric and I were full-blown adversaries. Unlike my time at Children's Place in Chesterfield, I was no longer the only Black student in my class. The Sumter public school district was almost evenly split between Black and White students, reflecting the city's population. Everyone essentially went to the same schools, unless you were White and wealthy—then you went to Wilson Hall, a private school in the town that should have had a WHITES ONLY sign plastered on it. Though my schools' racial demographics were split evenly, 90 percent of the teachers were White. This racial dynamic was true for my elementary school as well. And now that I was not the only Black student in my class, I noticed how teachers interacted with other students who looked like me. One of those students in particular was another Black boy named Eric. By looking at us, Eric and I were essentially the same. At that age, we were nearly the same height, size, and had practically the same skin complexion. But to say Eric and I had two completely different school experiences would be an understatement. Day in and day out, I was applauded for my behavior and achievement. For one, I was the only student in first grade who was allowed to select books from the fifth-grade section in our school's library because of my advanced reading ability.

Additionally, I was quiet, followed my teacher's instructions, and scored 100 percent on almost every assignment. The only thing that mattered to me was that my teacher was happy with my performance and behavior. I was an educator's dream. In contrast, Eric was less concerned with my teacher's approval. He was a jokester—a talkative, active, and playful first grader. And as much as I was applauded for my behavior, Eric was criticized for his. I was keenly aware of how Eric frustrated my teacher, and I took that frustration on as well. He simply would not follow the rules and made everything difficult for the class. Many of the other students in my classroom, both Black and White, also became increasingly frustrated with Eric, following my teacher's lead. But I was the most vocal. Eric's anger toward me and threats of violence were warranted, and to be honest, I felt similarly toward him. He was a living representative of everything I was beginning to comprehend society disapproved of—all the traits society condemned in my father. The anger I had toward Eric was, in many ways, the unexpressed anger I had toward my father.

ON ONE OCCASION during this time when I went to visit my father we planned to go to the park and get some Dunkin' Donuts, because those were the two things I wanted to do that day with him. I loved the glazed donuts and running in the park with my father like we used to when we lived together. As my father, his friend, and I left his apartment, we got in the car, and my father told me that we had to make a "few stops." During the car ride, I spent most of the time precociously chastising my father. I scolded him for using "bad" words when he talked to his friends; I even threw a pack of cigarettes out the window of his car after telling him, "Daddy, you shouldn't be smoking." He laughed and told me I needed to calm down, saying, "Remember, I'm still your daddy, boy." We made a stop and met up with a couple of people who had "packages" for him. I noticed a white powdery substance in Saran Wrap in the brown paper bags that he placed next to me. In my childish curiosity, I asked, "Is that marijuana, Daddy?" Shocked by my question, he and his friends began to laugh. "Huh," he said. "Boy, what do you know about marijuana? Who taught you about marijuana?" He never answered my question.

His friends were not allowed to speak to me the entire car ride. When any of his friends attempted to interact with me, he scolded them harshly, "Don't fucking speak to my son!"

Finally, after dropping his friends off with the packages, we arrived at Dunkin' Donuts. I was so excited. I wanted to get my longed-for glazed donut and then go to the park to play. However, when we got there, my father received a phone call on his car phone that made him irate. He began yelling, "Don't fucking play with me, motherfucker, I'll gut you like a fucking fish!" to the person on the other end of the phone. Meanwhile, I was in the background yelling at him from the passenger seat, "Daddy, hang up the phone! Stop cursing, now!" My yelling made him more upset with the person on the phone. "See, you got me cursing in front of my fucking son!" he yelled.

The adoration I once had for my father was fading. In my mind, he was turning into a "bad" person. I was so angry with his actions. I had been taught that drugs were bad, and I had a suspicion that my father was exposing me to them. Why was he doing this? I, for sure, knew that I was never going to act this way. I had already learned from people like my White kindergarten teacher that aggressive behavior was unacceptable. I was her "favorite student," as she would whisper to my mother at school dismissal. She was a sweet White woman whose approval I yearned for. And each day in her classroom, I received that approval, each day except the time I lost the spelling bee to a classmate, something that had never happened before. After realizing I misspelled the final word, I punched the wall and grunted out of anger.

In 2019, research conducted by a scholar from Columbia University indicated five-year-old boys with incarcerated fathers had substantially worse "non-cognitive readiness" in classrooms—things like staying on task, paying attention, and keeping emotions under control. I wonder if my bout of anger was linked to my father's absence and his previous incarceration? Nonetheless, I will never forget the look on her face the moment I erupted. It was a look of shock, horror, disapproval, disappointment, and discomfort. It was the look of a White woman encountering her worst perceptions of Black men. That look forever stayed with me, and I learned even if I was angry or felt like being aggressive, never to show it because important (White) people like my teacher would not like me anymore and would be uncomfortable. Therefore, my father's actions enraged my five-year-old self. He was everything that my White teacher disliked, everything I was beginning to hate, too. I was ready to leave. I did not want to spend any more time with him.

A few months later, my father was arrested.

————————

OVER THE LAST decade, educational experts have begun to widely use the phrase "school-to-prison pipeline" or "school-prison nexus" to acknowledge the connection to the disproportionate rate of minority students and students with disabilities experiencing harsher discipline policies in schools and later becoming incarcerated adults. Specifically Black and Latino students, and those students with disabilities (who are more often Black and Brown) are much more likely to be suspended or expelled from school than their White counterparts. Many scholars argue that these extreme disciplinary practices are directly tied to higher rates of juvenile delinquency and incarceration. I have always been uniquely positioned to see this trend play out in my own life. At the age of six, I was witnessing my father experiencing the criminal justice system once again—a Black man who had experienced harsh disciplinary practices in his schools. At the same time, I was witnessing my first-grade classmate get the brunt of similarly harsh disciplinary actions.

Over time, Eric's classroom behavior did not improve. He was often isolated in the classroom and received corporal punishment (paddling) from our principal, and even was suspended from time to time. Looking back, I am not convinced his daily behavior was much worse than my other classmates, though. However, when he brought a water gun to the class that resembled a real gun and threatened many students with it, myself included, he crossed a line he could not uncross. This action led to his expulsion from our school. I never saw or heard from Eric again.

If I was given the opportunity, I would love to reconnect with my first-grade classmate now as an adult. I want to know his story.

I frequently wonder what ever happened to him? How did his expulsion in first grade impact his life? Did he experience juvenile delinquency? Was he later incarcerated? The National Education Association states, "A suspension can be life altering. It is the number-one predictor—more than poverty—of whether children will drop out of school and walk down a road that includes greater likelihood of unemployment, reliance on social-welfare programs, and imprisonment." Another study, done by the Council of State Governments Justice Center, found that being suspended or expelled from school made a student three times more likely to come in contact with the criminal justice system within the next year.

Given what the research shows and what I know of how multiple school suspensions affected my father, I suspect Eric's journey might have been similar.

––––––––––

DURING THE MIDDLE of the school year in second grade, one day after school, my mother told me my father's yearlong trial was over. He had been sentenced. Over the past year, I knew my father was "in court" for "bad" things that he did, and we would find out how long he would have to be away from us when the judge finally made a decision. His charge was "conspiracy to possess and distribute cocaine and crack cocaine while using a firearm." During the lengthy trial to await sentencing, I remember sitting next to my mother, and she looked down at me and said, "Brian, you know your daddy has done some bad things. And when people do bad things, they get punished." She was preparing me for the blow she was about to give. "Brian, the judge said your daddy is going to have to be in prison for twenty-seven years," she said bluntly. As she said those words, I looked in shock and said back to her, "Twenty-seven years?" I paused and just stared at her. "I will be thirty-something when he gets out!" I said as my seven-year-old mind quickly tried to do the addition. I looked at my mother again, and the shock and grief finally took control. I began to cry hysterically.

As I sobbed, I said to my mother, "Twenty-seven years is a long time." I continued to cry as my mother consoled me. Though she was consoling me, I noticed my mother was not crying at all.

After I continued crying for many minutes, my mother took her arms from around me, grabbed my face, looked at me, and said, "Okay, Brian, that's enough. Stop crying. I know you are sad, but crying is not going to change it." I tried to stop the tears by wiping my eyes with my sleeves. It felt like my world had ended. *Is my father that bad to be taken away for twenty-seven years? Is that what's in store for my future?* If this is what happened when Black boys were "bad," then I knew for sure I would never be bad again.

The next morning, I woke up and went to school like any other normal day as if nothing had ever happened.

I OFTEN REFLECT on what was happening to me psychologically in these early years as I was beginning to matriculate through the public school system. My private pre-K and my public elementary school in Sumter could not have been more different. I realize now that my experiences were exactly as Baldwin and others described; it was early on in my life when the "shape of the oppression" of Black children like me was burgeoning in my mind. I was beginning to understand a "terrible weight" was on me and I couldn't shake it. What was consistent from pre-K through second grade was that in each of these classrooms those who looked like me and had similar life experiences were not celebrated. The same terrible weight was on my family, and I was beginning to internalize that this burden was something that we were all doomed to carry. The weight was crushing—at times it was even deadly.

"Ms. Reed, this weekend my uncle was killed. He was shot in the head, and then someone burned him in his car," I said to my first-grade teacher as I arrived at school that Monday morning. A couple of days earlier, my mother had informed me that my favorite uncle, Patrick, my father's younger brother, was murdered by someone he called his friend. I overheard the details of how it happened as the adults around me discussed the circumstances. I was shocked by what had happened and could not comprehend my feelings. My uncle would always call to see how I was doing, often check in on my mother and me, and buy me gifts even when I did not hear from my father. Yet again, I bore witness to the deadly consequences of what it meant to be Black in America and also what it meant to be Black in America's schools. All was happening at once: my father's incarceration, my uncle's murder, and my young mind attempting to wrap my head around seeing young Black boys like myself punished severely in school.

I was unclear about how people who looked like me were supposed to be treated. Eric had been expelled. My uncle had been killed. And my father was back in jail. I had a lot of confusion, anger, and frustration bottled up that I did not have an avenue to express. All I knew was that my school's approval felt reassuring.

I believe that American ills such as mass incarceration, poor life outcomes, and psychological despair are inextricably linked to our experiences in school. I can't help but think about how my father's thirteen years of school contributed to his twenty-seven year sentence. I can't help but think about how the school-to-prison pipeline impacts Black children, and other children at the margins, in our society today. And as I think about the hundreds of thousands of little Black children like Eric across America who, according to the Department of Education's 2020 statistics, are still much more likely to be suspended or expelled than their White classmates (three times more likely, to be exact), I also question what happens to their future. And I think about the future of all marginalized children who, though they are not being expelled or suspended, are experiencing the demoralizing mental impact of a different lived reality in school, that of repressing or hiding their true selves. Considering how the seeds of oppression planted in the minds of millions of Black children bloom into the mental distortions that deeply impact their life, starting and continuing through their thirteen-year school journey, I would argue that a twenty-seven year prison sentence, while long, is at least finite and visible as compared to the long-term negative psychological impacts of a thirteen-year sentence served in our public school system. And if this is true, which I firmly believe it is, then it's past time as a nation we start to do something about it.

CHAPTER 3

I Hate You

*Upon entering school in primary grades, Black children pos-
sess enthusiasm and eager interest; however, by fifth grade,
the liveliness and interest are gone, replaced by passivity
and apathy.*

—HARRY MORGAN, TAKEN FROM *COUNTERING THE
CONSPIRACY TO DESTROY BLACK BOYS*, 1983

THE CLARK DOLL TEST IS not the only study that reveals anti-
Black bias in America. Decades after the famed experiment,
numerous studies have shown a consistent anti-Black bias or,
more broadly, a pro-White affinity that persists in Americans of
all ages.

In a research study of over four million Americans conducted
by Harvard University's Project Implicit and published in 2019 by
the American Psychological Association, participants' explicit and
implicit attitudes showed significant preference for White people
over all racial groups, regardless of personal racial identity.

Current research continues to tell the same story, while as a society and education system, we refuse to acknowledge the story's
main plot. There is a consistent contempt for Black people and
other marginalized groups that is instilled in all Americans. Our

society refuses to fully acknowledge this truth, therefore allowing our education system the moral space to outright deny it. As I reflect back on my later elementary school years, it is interesting to track how the rotten fruit of this White supremacist ideology slowly bloomed, ripened, and decayed in my own life and the lives of the other children around me. And more importantly, I realize now that my continued matriculation through the American public school system played a leading role in this racial indoctrination.

OCTOBER 15, 2000

"I hate you. I hate you. I hate you. I hate you. I hate you," my nine-year-old hand wrote over and over again on the lines of my college-ruled paper. I penned those words at least fifty times in the letter I was writing to my father in federal prison. At the time, he and I would often write to each other, and each time we followed essentially the same script. He would tell me how much he missed me, how proud he was of me, and that he wished he could be home to hug me, come to my school performances, etc. Also, he always reminded me to make sure I was taking good care of my mother and being a little man for him. I would write him back and talk about school, how I missed him, and how I wished he were home. However, behind the politeness of my words, I concealed a deep rage. I was so angry with my father for being in prison, for abandoning me, for how I needed to make up for his "transgressions" each day. He was a representative of everything I was learning society hated—everything I was learning to hate. So, with this letter, I wanted him to really feel my pain. I was tired of bottling up my emotions. I wrote those three words continuously on the lines: "I hate you." Then after that cathartic ceremony, I erased all my writing. I wanted the paper to have the energy of my hatred, but I was too afraid to say those words to my father. Besides, my mother would have seen it and would not have allowed me to send it.

After erasing the phrases, I wrote my typical letter on the same college-ruled paper. I mentioned how I was making all As in school, how my teacher liked me, how I missed him so much, and how I could not wait to visit him. Lastly, I signed "Love always, your son Brian." We sent the letter, and a week or so went by until I received a call from my father. He called my grandparents' house and my mother answered. He spoke to her briefly, then she put me on the phone. He sounded distraught. He received my letter and saw in the background the faded words "I hate you." My nine-year-old attempt to erase the words was not as successful as I thought.

With frustration in his voice, he asked, "What's going on, Lil' Bit? Why did you write 'I hate you' in this letter?"

I denied that I wrote the words. He then said to tell him if I needed to talk to him. I said I was okay. He got off the phone irritated and defeated, and a part of me felt validated that he now knew my true feelings. My father was now becoming aware of the hatred I had for him, yet I was still unaware of my own self-hatred growing within.

———————

THIRD GRADE WAS a particularly tough year. I continued to excel academically and the teachers in the school liked me, but socially things were not ideal. Many of my Black classmates, especially the other Black boys, were experiencing school in a way that was in complete contrast to my experience. My class did not have only one student who had my first-grade classmate Eric's experience of school but instead, there were ten to fifteen struggling Black students. They were each being scrutinized daily by my White teacher for misbehaving, not following the rules, and not performing well academically. Conversely, I still listened to every word my teacher uttered, was quiet, well-behaved, and made good grades.

Interestingly enough, I do not recall my third-grade teacher being extremely nice to me despite my doing well. My relationship with her was quite different from the relationship that I had with my previous kindergarten, first-, and second-grade teachers. I often remember wishing that I had a "nicer" teacher for third grade. Was her personality just meaner than my other teachers? Or was it something more systemic?

Research shows that as Black and Brown American children get older, they are seen as more threatening and receive more biased treatment. One study conducted in 2020 showed that regardless of a person's stated beliefs about Black and Brown children, whether positive or negative, they more often misjudged the facial expressions of these youth as angry or aggressive. Further, according to the study "The Essence of Innocence," as Black youth get older, they are seen as less innocent than their counterparts in other racial groups. More specifically, starting at the age of ten, Black youth consistently are seen as significantly less innocent than their peers and are perceived as older. I hope that most of mainstream America has accepted the fact that we all come with biases, but I am sure we do not give enough consideration to how those biases impact the self-perception and development of our children. As I think about those other Black students who were in my class, I wonder how they must have felt to consistently be seen as "the problem" by my teacher. The difference between those students and myself was that she made it a point to let them know she didn't like them. Were these Black students only living out the perception of what my teacher expected of them or the expectations of a former teacher? To me, it felt like these students had a target on their backs that I, and everyone else, was keenly aware of. I knew that I didn't want that same target on me and I was willing to do whatever it took to avoid it.

Though my third-grade teacher was not the nicest, she did not punish me because I did everything she said. My unique experience in school further isolated me from my Black peers. It showed up most at social times like recess. At the time, I believed I would be the first neurosurgeon who was also an NBA player in history. It was easy in my nine-year-old mind. I would practice medicine in the off-season. So, with my dreams in tow, I frequently did what most of the other boys did during recess—I played basketball.

However, when I stepped onto the asphalt court, I was often not welcomed at all. Third-grade boys learning curse words to show how tough or cool they were relished hurling names at me like "punk," "nerd," "bitch," "faggot," "motherfucker." However, I have come to believe this hurling of insults was something more than boys coming of age. What I was experiencing reminded me of my father's experience with other Black kids his age who would often tease and ostracize him for speaking "too White" when he moved to South Carolina from his predominantly White schooling in Michigan. In a similar vein, I now realize, the boys spewed harsh words at me because I was an outsider, and therefore, a social target. They saw that the teachers at the school liked me, I made good grades, I was quiet, and my interests were different from theirs. My only genuine interest at the time was making my teachers happy and achieving academically in school.

Looking back, I think I must have been everything that those other Black boys despised. They had a negative experience in school, and here I was, someone who looked like them, being the teacher's pet. The name-calling did not deter me from wanting to play basketball, though, and so the names quickly turned to threats of violence. I can't count the number of times that boys tried to fight me on the playground. If I would score in basketball, play defense well, or stand up for myself, the threats would start. It seemed like it angered them that I, the outsider, wanted to participate in something they all shared. Though the threats of violence happened regularly, surprisingly, I never got into a fight. I was not necessarily afraid of the boys and would casually tell those who wanted to fight, "If you want to hit me, hit me." Deep down, I was hoping that one of the boys would hit me so I could express a mixture of hostility and self-hatred toward them and show them that I was tough. I would fantasize about punching them in the face, their noses and lips bleeding, choke-slamming them, or even stabbing them, leaving them bloodied on the asphalt basketball court. I wasn't a punk by any means, and I was hoping that I would be able to show them one day.

By the middle of the school year, I had given up trying to play with the other kids at recess. I was tired of the constant friction, and I began to become anxious every time I'd think about it. I started playing by myself. I would go to the last swing on the swing set and sit alone. As some of my classmates would come up to speak to me, I would tell them to leave me alone. My teacher noticed this behavior, and one day at school dismissal mentioned the change to my mother and asked if everything was okay. My mom reassured my teacher that I was fine.

When I would cry to my mother about my lack of friends at school, she'd tell me that it's okay and I didn't need anyone to be my friend. As long as I was being myself, that's all that mattered, she'd say. I held firm to her words and decided that I would no longer try to interact with boys who didn't want to befriend me. However, I was deeply sad. I was unhappy with my home life and depressed by my social experience at school. The only solace I had was that I made good grades and my teacher validated me. In time my sadness spiraled. I felt frustrated that my father was in prison, I did not have many friends at school, and though I was trying to do the "right" thing, it was causing me so much isolation from everyone else in my young world. I was beginning to hate who I was, and I wanted the pain to end.

There has been a significant rise in concern for youth mental health over the past few decades. In recent years, more light has been shed on the mental health crisis affecting many children of color in America and, most specifically, Black youth. According to a national advisory released by the US surgeon general in 2021, Black youth are much more likely to have depression, anxiety, and other adverse mental health challenges such as higher risk for suicide—and many argue that racism is the leading cause. This health crisis has become a national epidemic. When I think about this current epidemic in Black youth, my own mental health challenges over twenty years ago and the mental anguish of those Black and Brown children in generations before me, the common theme that emerges is how unmoved we are as a society by the suffering of Black children. Black suffering is consumable in this numbed America, and Black youth suffering is no exception. The stakes are high; in fact, they can even be deadly.

One night before my 8:30 P.M. bedtime, I was in the bathroom of my grandparents' house, washing up for bed. However, I was not bathing but rather sitting on the side of the tub crying while praying to God, asking him to kill me, to take my life. My nine-year-old mind was trying to find ways to end my emotional pain. Going to a Black Southern Baptist church every Sunday taught me that God was the creator of everything and HE had all the power, so surely, if I prayed to him to end my life, he would. After praying, I waited about five minutes, and nothing happened. I figured, then, that I needed to take matters into my own hands. I knew my mother or another family member would soon come to the bathroom to see why I was taking so long. In a hurry, I looked for something to accomplish the task before me. I saw a nail clipper with a metal nail file attached to it. I grabbed it, extended the file, and began to scrape it across my wrist aggressively. I had seen on television that people cut their wrists to kill themselves. To my disappointment, my scraping barely broke the skin. As I was scraping at my wrist and crying, I started to think of my mother and how sad she would be if she found me dead in the bathroom. I began to cry harder and I dropped the nail file. I struggled to complete my task at the thought of how devastated my family would be if I died. Though at the time I did not have much love for myself, the love that I had for my mother and the rest of my family, and them for me, made me abort the suicide mission. I prayed again for God to take my pain away. After putting away the nail clipper, I put rubbing alcohol on the tiny nick on my wrist, put my pajamas on, wiped my tears, came out of the bathroom, and went to sleep.

The *Journal of the American Medical Association* states that Black youth under the age of thirteen are twice as likely to commit suicide than their White peers. Three hundred and three. That is the number of Black children in America under the age of thirteen who committed suicide within the last two decades, and if you account for youth over thirteen the number rises considerably. The figure was recorded in 2015, so I can only infer that the number of Black youth suicides has since increased, and I often think about those lives needlessly lost. To make it worse, Black adolescents are the only racial/ethnic group that has seen a steady increase in suicide attempts over the last few decades. When I think back to my nine-year-old self in that bathroom, I desperately want to give the younger me a hug. I want to tell him that though he feels extreme isolation in school from his Black peers and is conflicted about the value of his racial identity within America and has not yet found a sense of joy in living, he one day will. Despite the efforts of a system to obstruct his joy, he will find it. Today as youth mental health has become a mainstream concern, researchers and parents alike are constantly searching for answers. Perhaps the path to the answers first begins with a question. That question being: What does our American school system teach our children about who they are, their worth, and their place in society? What does the American educational curriculum intentionally leave out that's harmful to historically marginalized youth? How do American schools directly contribute to these feelings of worthlessness and the epidemic of the rising Black mental health crisis?

I believe one area that can help us find these answers is dissecting how our public schools teach students about our history, and how Black students see themselves as a vital part of the American story.

———

"WE SHOULD LEARN about Madame C. J. Walker," I said to my White fourth-grade homeroom teacher.

She looked puzzled. "Who is that?" she responded.

I excitedly said, "She is the first self-made Black woman millionaire in America. She made her money by doing Black women's hair and making the hot comb straightening famous!" This was my attempt to articulate the basic knowledge I had about Madame C. J. Walker. Moments before, my teacher had asked the class for suggestions on who to learn about for Black History Month.

She said, "We always talk about Martin Luther King Jr., and I know there must be some other important Black people in history."

My classmates started to call out various names, and I thought Madame C. J. Walker was a great option. After I explained who Madame C. J. Walker was and her significance, my teacher responded by laughing and said, "I'm not sure there is anything important about a Black woman using a hot comb to straighten another

Black woman's hair." I was annoyed. *How can she say that?* I thought. Throughout my elementary years, my schooling had not affirmed my identity as a Black person at all. Most of the history taught did not speak about Black people but rather "great" White men and women in American history. When the curriculum focused on Black people, it was quite shallow, always mentioned our suffering and oppression, and was only during Black History Month.

And as for Black History Month, as an adult I have always had a love-hate relationship with the holiday. I am frustrated that Black history and other ethnic groups' rich stories are reduced solely to a month, week, etc. However, I understand the importance of acknowledging Black and minority contributions to a society that otherwise disregards them. Carter G. Woodson, the author of *The Mis-education of the Negro* and a key shaper of the framework for this book, is responsible for the origins of Black History Month, with the founding of national Negro History Week in 1926. National Negro History Week would later become Black History Month in 1976. However, like Black people's position in America, the "celebration" is disjointed, diminished, and is not an integral part of the American history we learn. And I think it has turned into more of a gimmick than anything else. Schools around the country are not legally required to provide curriculum coinciding with the holiday. Moreover, we can see from our current political climate that when Americans attempt to create more balance in teaching history and racial truths in this country, there is extreme pushback, for example the backlash to the *1619 Project*. As of June 2021, forty-two states have introduced measures to limit how race and discrimination can be taught in public schools. So, in reality my teacher's blatant disregard for my excitement about a Black prominent figure that she was unfamiliar with is only a mere reflection of America's blatant disregard of Black history.

But luckily for me, in fourth grade, my family had taken it upon themselves to tell me about great Black men and women. My uncle would tell me that ancient "Kemet" was the foundation of all modern human civilization and that every other race originated from Black people. My family and I would watch movies such as Spike Lee's *Malcolm X*, and I would learn how W. E. B. Du Bois was the first African American to graduate from Harvard. At home, I had more of a knowledge of my history, but it was barely mentioned in school. Therefore, highlighting Madame C. J. Walker seemed commonplace to me, but my teacher's response quickly brought me back to reality.

The educational system's hatred for Black and other historically marginalized students became clearer for me as I became painfully aware of the lack of proper representation in history instruction, but it wasn't only the curriculum that revealed it—it was also my school's internal structures and pathways.

Now that I was in fourth grade, things had changed drastically. Fourth grade was when my elementary school began "tracking" students based on their academic performance or, as one of my teachers would say, "based on students' IQ." Some form of tracking is still a common practice across most American schools today. Students would have a homeroom class that was not tracked where the teacher would only cover social studies and electives. However, reading, writing, math, and science were all tracked. As a result, my school placed me in all "challenge" classes for the highest performing students in the grade. In these classes, the majority of my classmates were White. There were a few other Black students, mostly girls, and often I was the only Black boy in my class. This structure further separated me from my Black male peers and led to more social isolation.

Another change that was evident to me in fourth grade was my relationship with my teachers. Third grade had introduced me to the idea that my teachers were not always going to be nice to me, but the fourth grade was when I first noticed my teachers had a negative reaction to me—a trend that would continue throughout my schooling. However, I still performed well and behaved, and I did not get in real trouble, so my fourth-grade teachers could not say much. In challenge classes, I noticed how much more freedom students had. I would often get excited to go to "challenge" because of the cool projects, activities, or field trips we participated in. It seemed as though our teachers were more relaxed with us and appeared happier than in other parts of the day when the students were not separated, and, candidly, there were more Black students. It also became much more apparent to me how much my White classmates could be mischievous and get a pass in these tracked classes. Frequently, they would not follow the teacher's instructions, but instead of being punished, it would merely be a nonchalant "slap on the wrist" from my teachers without real consequences. These actions frustrated me as I witnessed this behavior. Little did I know at the time that this would be a theme I would see throughout my educational experience. Regardless of the aspects I witnessed that were different between the challenge classes and regular classes, I still enjoyed my educational time there. I was challenged more academically and had more fun. We, as students, could have significantly more independence, and this was something I enjoyed.

In fifth grade, for the first time in my K–12 educational experience, I had a Black teacher, Ms. Hutchinson. When I think back on much of my educational career, I rarely had teachers who looked like me. Today, I understand the history behind this trend in America, where 80 percent of K–12 educators are White, though non-White students make up approximately 53 percent of the overall student population in the United States. A dismal 7 percent of educators are Black and are often grossly underrepresented in schools that have majority Black and Brown students. That history is deeply connected to the 1954 Supreme Court ruling to integrate schools which led to the mass firing, demoting, and pushing out of qualified Black teachers immediately afterward—some figures say roughly 38,000 Black teachers. I guess the blow of integration for mainstream White Americans at the time was too much and therefore they refused to also have their White children be taught by Black educators. Because of this history, it is no surprise that I barely saw any teachers that looked like me in my Sumter schools.

But in fifth grade, finally I had Ms. Hutchinson. She was my homeroom teacher and one of a couple of Black teachers in our entire school. She was new to the school that year but quickly received the reputation as one of the meanest teachers. You could hear her yelling down the hall at any point during the day. My other White teachers would often roll their eyes when they would hear Ms. Hutchinson's voice coming from her classroom. We students quickly picked up on our other teachers' feelings about her.

One day Ms. Hutchinson's emotions got the best of her when attempting to get our classroom to stop talking. Many of the students were continuing to chat, but a group of Black boys, in particular, were laughing in the back of the classroom. Out of anger, Ms. Hutchinson began to yell at them, demanding they stop laughing. When the boys continued to snicker, she then said, "You boys are just a bunch of ghetto gutter rats, who will probably end up in jail!" As she said this, the boys were unfazed. I imagine they had heard that or worse before and likely had become desensitized to the comments. However, I was bothered by her statements. Her words made me feel ashamed, even though she did not direct them to me. She said this to a group of Black boys who were like me, my cousins, uncles, or my father. *My father is in prison, so what would someone like her think of him?* My mind was racing, but I did not want to get yelled at or in trouble, so I remained silent and continued to complete my classwork.

THE TIME HAD come. Tonight was the highly anticipated Halloween carnival at my school. I had found the perfect pirate costume, black and white striped with an eye patch and black hat. My aunt, my mother, my little cousin, and I went to the festival to trick-or-treat. My cousin and I were excited to get the candy and to play the carnival games. As the evening progressed, I began to get annoyed with my eye patch and hat, so I took them both off. As we were walking by a group of White parents, one man snickered, "Oh, I see they are starting them out earlier and earlier nowadays." I knew exactly what he was implying. He was equating my black-and-white-striped outfit to a prisoner's uniform. My aunt overheard and told my mother; they were both angered and loudly said he was "stupid and ignorant" and walked away. I felt embarrassed. I did not like my costume anymore and became mad at my mother for picking it out. I asked my mother if we could leave. *Is this my fate?* I had been desperately attempting to escape my father's reality, but my world around me was trying to remind me every day that I was no different. Whether it was how my teachers behaved toward me and students who looked like me or harmful treatment by White parents in my school community, my environment told me again and again that Black people were less than. It felt like regardless of how hard I tried, there was nothing I could do to escape that reality.

"Who taught you to hate yourself from the top of your head to the soles of your feet? Who taught you to hate your own kind?" These words, directed to an audience of hundreds of Black people, loudly came from Malcolm X's mouth during a speech at the funeral of Ronald Stokes in May of 1962 in Los Angeles, California. Before saying these words, he condemned the United States for its lack of school integration though the Supreme Court ruling on *Brown v. Board of Education* happened eight years prior. He went on to say, "Who taught you to hate the race that you belong to, so much so that you don't want to be around each other?" I have listened to that speech many times over the years and have reflected on Malcolm's question, "Who taught you to hate yourself?"

As I think about my elementary school experience, I believe it was a breeding ground for the hatred that Malcolm spoke of. Though I had experienced the consequences of systemic racism in our American society before entering elementary school, my time there cultivated, developed, and normalized the hatred. From the mistreatment of Black students in my classrooms, to the hatred Black boys had for me and I for them, to the lack of positive, liberatory teaching of Black history and Black contributions to the United States, to the academic tracking that once again segregated students by race beginning in fourth grade, to discriminatory comments made by teachers, all of these elements taught hate. They taught the Black students to hate who they were and see themselves as less in a society built on their oppression. They taught the

Black students that they were second-class citizens in schools meant to educate them. They taught them that being around one another was not a positive circumstance but rather a negative one. They taught that suppression was the only way to survive.

So, if I had the privilege to be in the audience on that day in Los Angeles in 1962, and respond to Malcolm's question "Who taught you how to hate yourself?" I would answer that our American schools are one of the biggest teachers of self-hatred to Black and Brown people in this country. And, in my experience, it begins as early as elementary school. I would go on to argue that in any good lesson, you should be able to see the outcomes of what was taught. By looking at the state of Black students based on statistics by the time they enter middle school, the lesson in self-hatred is one of the best our educational system teaches.

PART II

Secondary Education

CHAPTER 4

United States of America v. Brian A. Fuller

I began by saying that one of the paradoxes of education was that precisely at the point when you begin to develop a conscience, you must find yourself at war with your society. It is your responsibility to change society if you think of yourself as an educated person.

—JAMES BALDWIN, "A TALK TO TEACHERS," 1963

SEPTEMBER 22, 2002

As I was looking over my mother's shoulder, I read the words *United States of America v. Brian A. Fuller.* They hovered on the screen of our desktop, courtesy of the Internet in its infancy. When I saw those words, I was shocked. In disbelief, I exclaimed, "The entire United States is going against him. He's never going to win!" My mother laughed and explained that all federal cases were labeled this way: the United States versus the person charged with a federal crime. She explained that my father was in federal prison; therefore, his case was a federal case, which is why the court documents read that way.

I was somewhat relieved but still a bit confused. My father had been in the process of appealing his conviction, and once again, in

47

September of 2002, his appeal was denied. My mother was familiar with going online to see the court documents that recorded the court's denial of his appeal. In fact, we had sent copies of my report cards and scholastic awards to federal judges in hopes of convincing them that I needed my father at home.

However, this was the first time I had seen the words *United States of America v. Brian A. Fuller* on the documents. Looking back now, seeing those court documents was significant in my development at a critical period, the middle school years.

I had recently come off the heels of an elementary school environment that reinforced the idea that the educational system was not always in favor of students of color like me. Time and time again, I witnessed the mistreatment of my fellow Black classmates and I saw firsthand how many of them fell through the cracks of the system. At the same time, I desperately tried to escape this same fate by doing everything I thought was appropriate and acceptable by my school's standards. I did not yet realize that these experiences were not unique to me and the students in my city of Sumter. Instead, I, along with all students, was a part of a much larger ecosystem that was producing the same results as my experience.

With that in mind, maybe my initial question to my mother was more than an eleven-year-old's attempt to understand federal cases. Perhaps my question was a valid foreshadowing of what it meant to be a Black student in America. If the entire United States were against my father, or rather, all of us—Black and marginalized students—then how could we ever think we were going to win? And as my social consciousness continued to develop in middle school, this question would become even more pertinent.

MANY PEOPLE, INCLUDING myself, look back on middle school and feel some lingering sense of anxiety. Middle school has always been a tricky age for young people and often is the least sought after school age to teach. Many have often referred to middle school as an "educator's nightmare." Not only is this the stage in life where hormone fluctuations are making young people's emotions change with the same ferocity of a person experiencing pregnancy, it is also a time that adolescents, as Baldwin put it, are truly starting to develop consciousness about the world around them, leading them to challenge that world in significant ways. Most of us can remember how we were as adolescents, and some of you reading these words may be educators or parents currently interacting with this particular age group on a daily basis. Without a doubt, middle school is rough.

But, going further, I would argue the middle school stage is the most dangerous time to be Black or a student on the margins in America's public education system. What happens during this time period has been shown to have serious implications for the rest of a student's educational life. According to a report by the Brookings Institution, a DC-based national policy research organization, "Middle school appears to be the chronological dividing line for when African American suspension rates escalate."

As I have already mentioned in the previous chapter, as Black and Brown children grow older, they are seen as less innocent and disciplined more harshly. Another study, conducted by the University of Texas at Austin, showed that Black and Brown students are suspended the most in middle schools as compared to high schools and elementary schools. Further, the study revealed, Black and Brown students have been shown to develop a strong lack of trust in authority figures and their ability to administer discipline fairly or equally as compared to their White counterparts. "Middle school students of color who lose trust in their teachers due to perceptions of mistreatment from school authorities are less likely to attend college even if they generally had good grades." This unequal treatment leads to lasting perceptions for students, and those perceptions impact academic success and aspirations.

But I did not need research to tell me the facts; I only had to reflect back to my sixth- to eighth-grade years in Sumter, South Carolina.

———

LIKE IN MANY American cities, multiple elementary schools in Sumter funneled into three middle schools. I was nervous to enter sixth grade in this larger educational environment. I had heard rumors of more fights and kids getting bullied. Also, I heard that teachers would no longer be as understanding with students. I did not know what exactly to expect going in, but I was determined to be "cooler" than I was in my younger years. I craved a different experience. I was tired of being called names, not having many friends, and not being seen as one of the cool kids.

Like most middle school-aged students, social acceptance was vital to me. Based on my past academic success, I was tracked into all honors courses, which were mostly White, but I deeply wanted to be accepted by my Black peers. Tired of the social isolation I felt in elementary school, I set out to make friends with Black students at this new, "tougher" school in one of the only racially integrated classes in my schedule—my homeroom class. Notably, I befriended two Black boys, Carlos and Alain, who were a lot more socially accepted than I was. They did not go to my elementary school, so my stigma as a social outsider was unknown to them. Alain was an up-and-coming middle school football and basketball star. All the other boys wanted to be his friend, and all the girls in the school had a crush on him. Carlos was quieter, but he had a reputation of being cool and well respected. With these new, tight-knit friends, my social status with Black peers skyrocketed. Though some Black boys from my past life in elementary school still taunted me, my newfound friends defended me as if the disrespect had been directed toward them.

My personality was transforming, too. For Black boys in South Carolina, masculinity was everything, and the parameters around it were highly rigid. My soft, pleasant, nonthreatening demeanor, though my safeguard with White teachers, was not appreciated by many other young Black men. For them, the tougher you were or, at least, the tougher you were perceived to be, the more socially accepted you became. Any deviation from this structure meant sure social isolation and ridicule. So, I decided to change, to get "tough."

Toughness was social currency for most Black youth in my middle school. If I were to become more accepted by my peers, I would need to embrace violence and aggression. So, after school, I would immerse myself in depictions of violence. My younger cousin and I would search for "worst hood fight videos" on streaming platforms like LimeWire. Also, by the time I was in seventh grade, my friends and I were obsessed with the new up-and-coming rapper 50 Cent. Aside from being a talented rapper, he had infamously been shot nine times—a badge of toughness and authenticity that we seventh graders respected. As we saw it, violence was power and this power represented the possibility of freedom from oppressors. His encounters with the criminal justice system only built him up in our minds as an outlaw rebel and added to his aura. While most Americans saw 50 Cent and other Black men like him as criminals, we saw him as a hero—someone who had reclaimed his power in society and had broken free from its efforts to capture and restrict Black people. This was the first time in my life that I considered a Black man behind bars might be powerful.

Americans, and authority figures specifically, see Black masculinity as inherently dangerous and criminal. As Michelle Alexander and other scholars have illustrated in their work, after the "emancipation" of enslaved people in America, to uphold the status quo Black people needed to be placed back in captivity. And so the Black slave became the Black criminal. Black captivity was our real American history and is still our present-day lived reality.

It was in middle school that I began to learn more definitively about the longstanding Black American dilemma this reality presents. I began to see I could choose social well-being and fall into the preconceived notions of Black criminality my White teachers held, notions common to many Americans and that persist today. Or I could embrace the traits that made me acceptable to my White teachers, the very same ones that would then segregate me from my Black peers. I had already started to understand this critical trade-off in my primary school experience and knew that missteps could result in social exile.

Performative toughness, though respected in the context of Black masculine life, has real-life consequences. I saw these consequences with my father and my uncles early on and I saw how the cycle continued with my little half brother who during his teenage years didn't see the option to back down from a fight and was shot six times in the dispute. All of the Black men in my life and those I idolized from afar needed to be tough so they could receive respect, the respect that in our realities also meant freedom.

On the other hand, even in the instances where Black youth are not fighting for some arbitrary "respect" or performing "toughness," they are still met with the same narrative of inherent guilt, the absurd conclusion that they are worthy of punishment for just being. Take, for instance, the multitude of examples in America of young Black people who were innocent but assumed guilty: the Central Park Five, Tamir Rice, Latasha Harlins, Trayvon Martin, and Emmett Till. These young Black people were never granted the American value of "innocent until proven guilty" but rather were guilty from the onset. This presumption of guilt cost them their lives.

Our schools perpetuate this warped value of guilt before innocence for Black and Brown students even in many instances when there is no danger or disobedience at all.

I saw this with a few of my own teachers in middle school.

My first serious issue with a teacher was in seventh grade. I had a White male teacher, Mr. Davis, for Honors Math, and I was one of four students of color in the room. I was close friends with two of them, another Black boy named James and an Asian boy named Patrick. Patrick often hung out with the Black students. Looking back, I could only imagine how difficult it must have been to be Asian in Sumter's schools. Because most of the students were predominantly Black and White, there was no place socially or otherwise where Asian students' identities were even recognized. Most Asian students either assimilated to the Black student culture or the White student culture. We students would even say, "oh, he's a Black Asian" or "she's a White Asian" as a way to describe them. Patrick was a "Black Asian," and he, James, and I were friends.

However, it seemed my math teacher was not a huge fan of our group of friends or of us being in his class. He would often become snarky with us and not helpful if we had questions concerning the classwork. Anytime the three of us would chat with one another, as seventh-grade boys will do, he would reprimand us in a way that was far beyond that of his reaction to the other White students in the class. I noticed this biased behavior, so I began to challenge him often. I did not like his inequitable treatment of me and my friends, and I was not afraid to speak up.

My outspokenness came to a head when he accused me of lying about completing a homework assignment. I was typically meticulous about my work, but on one morning early in the school year, as Mr. Davis was walking around collecting assignments, I noticed that I did not have my name on the top of the worksheet. I quickly wrote my name and date on the paper as he was walking up to my desk. When he arrived at my desk, he said, "Mr. Fuller, I can't give you credit for homework that you didn't complete at home."

I was baffled and responded, "What are you talking about? I just wrote my name and date on the paper. You saw me. I did this work at home."

He replied, "I saw you rushing to complete the worksheet before I arrived at your desk."

Becoming more irritated, I said, "How could I complete this entire assignment in ten seconds? You're not making any sense. If I didn't do my homework, I would tell you—I'm not afraid of you."

He aggressively said back to me, "I'm not giving you credit for the assignment. End of discussion," and walked away. As he was leaving, I heard him say through laughter, "I see the smoke coming from your paper from your attempt to write so fast."

His condescending words and dismissive attitude infuriated me because he accused me of something that wasn't true, and gave me an unwarranted zero on a homework assignment I had carefully completed.

Frustrated, I said, "Oh, is the smoke you're seeing the same smoke that's destroying your lungs every day?" It was a known fact that between classes (and often during them) this particular teacher would walk outside to take a cigarette break. He would easily go through a pack of cigarettes a day. Enraged by my incisive comment, he turned to me and yelled, "Get out of my classroom!" to which I responded, "Gladly."

While this incident was unfortunate, it turned into an unfair pattern of punishment. From then on, each week, I would spend at least two days outside his classroom. He would kick me out for minor infractions. It seemed as if he were looking for reasons to toss me out. If I whispered to ask my neighbor a quick question, I was kicked out. If I came inside the classroom laughing with other students, I was kicked out. Essentially, it got to the point where I felt as if I even looked at him the wrong way, I was kicked out. I would feel embarrassed standing in the hallway next to his class-room door for the forty-five minutes of his class period as other students and the occasional teacher would walk by the room. Luckily for me, math came reasonably easy at the time, so despite often being out of the classroom, I still excelled in the class.

This sort of targeted behavior from teachers continued in eighth grade with my Honors English teacher, Ms. Bennett. She was an older White woman who, at the beginning of the course, I genuinely liked. I always excelled in English, so I was excited to be in her class. For the first major paper in her class she asked us to research and write about a social justice issue of our choosing. She told us we could tackle any topic of our choice so long as it was a significant social justice issue, and she would personally be screen-ing each of our subjects before we began writing. I was ecstatic about this project. I was thrilled I finally had free rein to write about a topic I was passionate about. I thought this paper would be an excellent opportunity for me to shed light on mandatory minimum sentencing in our criminal justice system, the same sys-tem that impacted my father and so many other Black and Latino men like him.

I submitted my topic for her review with my rationale. A few days later, she told the class that she generally was pleased with the topics but that "some of us" had turned in topics that "did not make sense" or "were not social justice related." When she returned my topic submission, she told me I needed to choose another topic because she "did not understand my example." I realized that among my classmates, I was the only one whose topic was not approved. I was confused when she told me she did not understand my topic because, to my knowledge, I was crystal clear about mandatory minimums and why it was a significant social justice issue in the United States. I even had my mother and uncle read over it at home before turning it in to my teacher.

At the end of the class that day, I asked her about my topic choice. She started by saying that she had "no clue" what I was referring to. *What were mandatory minimums?* I told her that mandatory minimum sentencing resulted in Black people being incarcerated for significantly more time than White people for essentially the same nonviolent crimes. I went on to say there was an extreme sentencing disparity between crack cocaine and powder cocaine which reflects the race of who generally sells and uses the forms of the drug. She looked at me indignantly, as if I had spoken to her about an issue that threatened her own livelihood in some strange way. She then said, "That is not a social justice issue. I've never heard of that. And there is nothing wrong or unjust about people getting arrested for crimes they committed. Choose a different topic." I was irritated that she so quickly dismissed what I was saying.

After that interaction, our relationship changed. I wrote my paper on a topic that did not interest me as much, but I listened to what my teacher had asked me to do. However, oddly enough, when she returned our assignments, she told me that she had lost the paper that I turned in a couple of weeks earlier. She proceeded to tell me that she "looked everywhere" and asked me if I was sure I turned it in. My paper was the only one in the class that she lost. I was in disbelief. I told her that of course I turned in my assignment, and my classmates immediately began to corroborate that I turned it in, which forced her to agree that I did. She then said that she "simply had lost it," and I would need to turn it in again. She told me she hoped I had saved my work. In my mind, I knew I had not. I had one family computer at home used by multiple people so after printing, I removed my assignments to free up storage and to not slow down our already slow computer. I told my teacher that I did not think I saved my project, especially after two weeks.

She replied, "The responsible thing to do is always save your assignments."

By this point, I was highly annoyed because she was suggesting that if I could not reproduce an assignment I turned in, I would have to redo it to receive a grade, or else I would get an F. I responded to her in my irritation, saying, "Well, I didn't expect my teacher to be irresponsible and lose my paper."

The next day, I returned and informed her that I had not saved my assignment. She then told me I would have to redo it. After a back-and-forth between us, my mother got involved, which eventually led to my teacher counting my lowest-scoring paper as a proxy for my major assignment for that semester. With this incident and what I had experienced with my math teacher, I was beginning to realize that the system might not be on my side as much as I had previously thought.

———

VISITS WITH MY father were happening more often. He had moved from a West Virginia federal correctional institution to one in Petersburg, Virginia. He was now only a four-hour drive away. My mother believed it was important that I maintained a relationship with my father, so we would visit him one weekend out of each month.

These visits were generally enjoyable and helped me build a stronger relationship with my father. The hatred I once had for him became less pronounced as I started to talk with him more about his world views, and my views of Black criminality were shifting. We would spend the hours in the visitation room discussing his newfound beliefs as a member of the Moorish Science Temple of America—a religious organization founded in the 1920s promoting Black unity and civic engagement that influenced the start of the Nation of Islam years later. My father told me that as

African Americans, we were the descendants of the Moors and that we should claim it as our birthright and nationality. In his words, the classification of "Black" was a term given to us in America to strip us of our rights and make us second-class citizens. He would go on further to say that the temple believed our religion of origin was Islam. My father had become a leader within the movement in his prison and was even appointed as a "Grand Sheik"—leading the teachings to fellow members in his prison. We would often debate about his newly acquired views as they were far from what I was exposed to at St. John's Baptist Church with my grandparents every Sunday. However, though I did not fully buy into all the new ideas my father was sharing with me, I remember feeling a sense of pride about him in these conversations that I had not felt since preschool. I was proud he was a leader among the men in the prison, and more importantly, this was the first time I had truly seen him with a firm conviction and sense of pride in himself.

At the same time, I was beginning to develop a sense of pride about my father. I became more critical of the world I lived in. My father and I would talk about his case and how "the system" convicted him on a mandatory minimum sentence for crack that disproportionately impacted Black and Latino men—giving them significantly longer sentences than for other nonviolent crimes. In 2002 alone, 63 percent of the incarcerated adult population in the United States were Black and Latino. Of the 63 percent, 25 percent were incarcerated for nonviolent drug crimes. In our visits, my father and I would discuss how the United States government was not in favor of Black people having the same liberties as White citizens. As we talked about these concepts, I would reflect on what I was experiencing in middle school.

I was battling for acceptance with people who looked like me and battling with teachers to not be seen as criminal. *If my father is so right, why are God and the universe placing him and men like him in prison?* I did not know what fully to believe but had learned from my own experience that Black and other marginalized children like me were treated differently in schools and society. From these conversations, I knew I would no longer stand by and let that mistreatment happen without challenging the system.

———————

JAMES BALDWIN, FOR me, has been a brilliant guiding force in thinking about the psychological implications of being a Black student in America and as a result, how one constantly wrestles with the dire realities of their world. Especially meaningful to me is a quote from his 1963 talk to a group of teachers delivered at Columbia University, where he articulates the paradox of education and what transpires as one "develops a conscience." He concludes that once you develop a conscience in your educational journey "you must be at war with your society."

His word choice of *war* stands out to me for many reasons. Most notably is that when one is at war with something or someone, the war is never one-sided. War always involves at least two parties actively engaging in battle. So if being educated as a Black or marginalized person in society means you must find yourself at war with your society, it must also mean you have realized that the same society is already at war with you.

I firmly believe middle school is where one begins to develop this conscience, as Baldwin puts it, and starts to wage war against their society, both consciously and subconsciously. Battle in the war as a marginalized student shows up subconsciously as violence toward one another, toward other non-marginalized students, toward the school environment, and leads to disengagement from learning altogether. Whereas the same battle shows up consciously when marginalized students directly challenge the system and authorities, call out their hypocrisies, their injustices, and rebel against the system's narratives for them. Regardless of whether the marginalized student is fighting the war subconsciously or consciously, their opponent, the education system, always meets them with the same response—extreme violence and suppression. And I, like millions of other students, was met with the system's response once I began to develop a conscience and began to wage my own war.

"ARE YOU CALLING me a racist?" My six-foot-four, White male principal said as he towered over me with his eyes stretched and his face beet red.

I responded, "I'm not calling you anything. I just did an experiment, and the result speaks for itself."

My friends and I had just run an experiment to prove that my middle school's administration was discriminating against Black students. It began when we were sitting in the lunchroom during eighth grade. I was saying how frustrated I was that White boys never got in trouble for having their shirts untucked, but we Black boys were always punished harshly. The school policy was that boys had to tuck in their shirts as a part of the school dress code. They told us that tucking in our shirts was to keep students safe as it would reveal if a student was carrying a weapon on them. There had already been a few violent incidents involving box cutters at the high school and threats of gun violence, so our district was taking extra precautions. Although they had instituted a standard dress code policy, the way that school leadership administered it was not standardized at all. The only students who truly were held accountable for the policy were Black students. Time and time again, I would witness my Black friends get in trouble for having their shirts untucked, even if by mistake, while my White male friends would never get consequences. Many of my Black friends had received referrals and sometimes even suspensions because of their shirts being untucked.

I was frustrated with what was happening, and I decided to take action. I wanted to prove to the administration that they were indeed biased against Black young men. My Black friend James was already eating with me, and he agreed to participate in the experiment I had in mind. Now all we needed was a White male to participate as well. I thought of our friend Henry because he was a popular sports player. He played football and I trusted him. So, I asked Henry to walk past the administrators' table first with his shirt untucked to see if the principal or assistant principal would stop him.

As we planned it, Henry walked past the table with his shirt un-tucked, and no one at the administrators' table said anything. The eight of us watching at our lunch table were now giggling. Henry made eye contact with us, and we motioned for him to walk past the table again. He walked past the administrators' table again with his shirt untucked and still, there was no comment. My prin-cipal and assistant principal were doing what they almost always had done with White students—easily overlooking their trans-gressions.

Henry came to our table, and we told him to go back again but this time loiter around, forcing them to notice him. He went back to the administrators' table and stood around for a while until my principal said to him, "Mr. Richardson, tuck your shirt in, sir. You know better than that." Henry snickered and tucked in his shirt and came back to our table.

Now it was James's turn. James untucked his shirt and walked past the administrators' table. This time not only was James stopped immediately, but the principal demanded that he come to him. "Mr. Kelly, tuck in your shirt. No, come here! You know better than to walk around with your shirt untucked. I should write you up for this. What's wrong with you?"

The newly hired Black assistant principal chimed in. "It's ridicul-ous," she said. Because of the extreme difference in my principal's response to James versus his response to Henry, James could not hold in his laughter. As the principal was chastising him, he began to chuckle. As he started to laugh, our principal became increas-ingly infuriated.

"Oh, so you think this is funny?" he exclaimed. "You think my rules are a joke? Come with me to my office now!"

We all were witnessing our friend about to land in serious trouble. I told the group that we needed to intervene. So, we all jumped up and ran over to the principal and James. I began to ex-plain our experiment. I went on to say that James only laughed because he had reacted more harshly to him than to Henry. As I revealed our social experiment to the principal while my friends stood in the background, he became visibly angry. He then accused me of calling him a racist. I assured him that I did not call him anything but that we only conducted an experiment. He then proceeded to say that his job was "serious," and he didn't have time for "students to waste with silly experiments." He then told the other students they could go but demanded Henry, James, and myself come to his office as we were in "big trouble."

Henry was visibly nervous as he did not want anything to jeopardize his eligibility to play football. James seemed a bit uncomfortable. I was angry. This moment was the first time in my school history that I was in the principal's office for something negative. My adrenaline was pumping. I felt like his reaction was extreme and proved the point that he was racist. As we walked into his office, he said, "All right fellas, I need to call your parents because this is ridiculous that y'all are wasting my time with this. So, who's up first?"

James and Henry looked even more nervous. Knowing my mother would be on my side and to show my principal his threats were not fazing me, I said, "You can call my mom first," and proceeded to give him her cell phone number. The principal spoke with my mother first, then called Henry's and James's parents and told us that he would decide on our consequences for our "unacceptable behavior."

While the three of us were in the office, the assistant principal was researching our student profiles. She knew both Henry and James because they were athletes, but she was unfamiliar with me. As I was walking out of the office, she said, "…and you're supposed to be an honors student—supposedly making good grades? No other behavioral incidents? Well, there's nothing honorable about what you're doing now. I'm surprised you're an honors student." Her antagonizing words made me livid. However, I calmly ignored her and kept walking.

The principal later said that because I had orchestrated the experiment, I would be the one to get the brunt of the punishment—alluding to a decision to suspend me. That evening when I got home, I told my mother, my aunts, and my grandparents the details of what happened earlier that day. My mother was furious to hear my account of the events. My mother said she was proud of how I handled the situation and what I did. My grandparents were not as supportive of the experiment but said that I was not disrespectful, so I did not deserve punishment from the school. It felt reassuring to have the support of my family.

The next day everyone in the school was gossiping about what had happened. In an effort to find more dirt on me, the principal had come to my eighth-grade teachers about the incident. However, to my surprise, many of my teachers banded together in support of me. My White homeroom teacher mentioned to me that she had heard what happened, but she thought I was an excellent student, and she would say that to anyone who asked her and that "no one can make her say different."

Also, my White male Algebra I teacher, who was the father of one of my classmates and friends from my honors classes, mentioned that he heard about the situation but that all he said was, "Brian is a good kid and very smart. Not a troublemaker at all." It made me feel good to know that my teachers supported me even if the administration did not.

A couple of days later, my mother had an in-person meeting with both the principal and assistant principal. In that meeting, my mother informed them that she and my grandfather knew our district superintendent—a Black woman who was my mother's professor many years prior and known in the community. She asked them why they never thought to ask us students why we wanted to do the experiment or why we felt a racial disparity in the school's discipline practices. My mother then told the assistant principal that her words as I was leaving the office were uncalled for and immature. I believe as a result of them realizing my mother's strong connection with their boss and their unprofessionalism in the moment, they abruptly agreed with my mother and apologized. Then, they told her that the assistant principal would apologize to me for her antagonizing behavior, but the apology never came. In the end, I was not formally punished, and the incident died down.

MIDDLE SCHOOL WAS pivotal for me as a Black student in America. And, as I previously articulated, these years are the most dangerous for American students at the margins. For me, these were the years when I first dared to challenge the society I lived in. These were the years I questioned why the system produced specific outcomes that I had witnessed throughout my childhood. These were the years when I realized the system was waging warfare against me and I with it. And these were the years when I first began to consider how I might change my society, as Baldwin suggested.

When I think about this time period, I often wonder, how do students on the margins navigate this system when a parent or caretaker is not able or available to advocate for them, as mine was? What consequences do students face when they speak out against the racist disciplinary practices of their school administrators? I know that incidents like the ones I shared in my personal story are still consistently occurring today, based on data reported by many public schools.

Whether due to hormones, new academic and social challenges, or the growing pains associated with becoming a young teen, the stakes are much higher for American students once they enter middle school. Further, what I hope the general American public begins to increasingly realize, is the fact that middle school is a crucial period in the story of our American way of schooling, not just a period to endure or survive. The middle school period is when, I believe, Black and other marginalized children fully face the hard truth of the clear divide in our education system and, by extension, in our country. Once faced with this truth, these same students then have to choose how to react, how to react to a world that is violently disempowering them daily. The choices these students make, choices forced upon them by the White supremacist nature of our educational system, will carry them through the rest of their educational journey and inevitably their lives. My questions are: How can our educational system stop putting Black and other marginalized students in this position? How can American middle schools move from disempowering students to empowering them?

Such a revolution starts with reexamining how we discipline students, track them, and support them in the development of their critical thinking and social consciousness. Rather than harshly punishing students, middle school teachers and leaders could set aside any assumption of criminality before they engage with any individual. Rather than isolating students in tracked programs, middle schools could identify the talents of all students and allow them to explore the abilities they naturally possess. Rather than discourage the instinct to challenge authority, schools could promote critical thinking and cultivate a healthy, challenging, and skeptical stance toward the world. Rather than suppressing identities, they could embrace the cultural, ethnic, and racial differences we have in our schools. By doing all of this, middle schools would allow students to reimagine what a world could look like outside of America's assumed racial caste system. If we rethink, restructure, and revolutionize how we do middle school in this country, our educational system would no longer be at odds with our Black and marginalized students, but rather be a crucial partner in their empowerment.

CHAPTER 5

Oh, the Places You Will Go!

The current system of control depends on black exceptional-
ism; it is not disproved or undermined by it.
—MICHELLE ALEXANDER, *THE NEW JIM CROW*, 2010

O UR EDUCATIONAL SYSTEM, LIKE OTHER oppressive structures
in America, is a deceitful one. I believe its biggest deceit is the
idea of meritocracy, the idea that hard work, intellect, and perseverance are the keys to success and therefore anyone can attain
success, regardless of race, social class, or any other identifier. This
falsehood is upheld daily by exceptional minority students, like
my younger self, who "defy all odds" and succeed. These students
end up in the high-performing classes, they perform well, and
they prove, it is supposed, that anyone can achieve. This flawed notion leads those who believe in the current system to conclude
that if the majority of the other Black or traditionally marginalized students are not achieving, it is solely by their own doing and
has nothing to do with the structure of the "colorblind" system.
In other words, the success of those few minority students in navigating the system actually acts, on the whole, as a painfully
invalidating barrier to the many other students who attest the
same system is actively countering their ability to thrive.

Scholars, such as Michelle Alexander and others, refer to this phenomenon as the flawed nature of "exceptionalism" and specifically "Black exceptionalism." As they put it, Black exceptionalism is one of the key elements that continues to uphold a racially oppressive system. I believe high school is one of the points in our education system where the notion of exceptionalism and Black exceptionalism is most fortified, as one can see how few Black and marginalized students enroll in Advanced Placement and other highly selective high school courses across the country. Of students enrolled in AP courses, about 52 percent are White while only 9 percent are Black, according to the Department of Education. My high school experience was especially filled with the Black exceptionalism myth as it intersected with the rise of a new, young Black presidential candidate, Barack Hussein Obama.

JANUARY 20, 2009

> *It's been too hard livin'*
> *But I'm afraid to die*
> *'Cause I don't know what's up there*
> *beyond the sky*
> *It's been a long, a long time comin'*
> *but I know a change gon' come*
> *Oh yes, it will!*

At 5:30 A.M., my mother, uncle, aunts, cousins, and what felt like at least a hundred other people melodically chanted "A Change Is Gonna Come" on a crowded city bus in Washington, DC, as we drove toward the United States Capitol. We were all here to witness the inauguration of the first Black president, Barack Hussein Obama. Sam Cooke's famous song was an appropriate soundtrack for this historic moment in our nation's history.

My father's older sister Charnelle had snagged two tickets to the inauguration ceremony through her workplace. She gave them, respectfully, to my grandparents. However, my grandma decided it was more important for the young Black men in her family to witness this pivotal American moment. She wanted to go; but we *needed* to go. So, my father's youngest brother, Terrance, and I received the tickets. I was ecstatic.

The majority of my family was there for the historic weekend. To be in DC during those few days was a dream come true. People were hugging one another and expressing love and bliss everywhere we looked. Tears of joy and laughter flowed. The atmosphere was filled with euphoric energy.

Once we arrived at the gates leading to the Capitol, my uncle and I went to get in line while the rest of my family waited outside, ready to watch the ceremony from the massive screens towering above the streets. I had never seen lines so long, and also, I had never been in weather so cold. My inauguration ticket stated, "Admit Bearer to West Front of Capitol."

This inauguration was the fifth coldest in history. The projected high temperature for the afternoon was twenty-eight degrees Fahrenheit with a wind chill that made it feel much colder. And boy, could I feel it. I had piled on three of my uncle's coats, sweatpants, and jeans and stuffed hand and feet warmers I bought from street vendors into various nooks and crannies.

Standing in that line was brutal. But as I looked around, I saw, standing in unity, men, women, gay people, straight people, Asian Americans, Black Americans, White Americans, Indian Americans, Latinos, and many more identities and cultures that make up our pluralistic society. I imagine this was a similar feeling to what Malcolm X wrote about when he visited Mecca, Saudi Arabia, for the first time and recounted, "Never have I witnessed such sincere hospitality and overwhelming spirit of true brotherhood as is practiced by people of all colors and races here." I was in awe. I also saw the elderly, individuals in wheelchairs, and many others in physical conditions much different from my own, all waiting patiently in the same line to witness this historic moment. I thought, *How could they possibly be enduring this cold and physical strain?* I realized I had no reason to complain. As one elderly Black woman in a wheelchair told me, she had "waited all her life for this moment," and she wasn't going to miss it.

After hours of waiting in line and then waiting again once we entered the gates, the moment had at last come. Barack Hussein Obama was being sworn in and I, along with the thousands and thousands in the crowd, were elated. I let out a cheer. I could not clap because my hands were too numb, but the numbness in all my extremities was irrelevant at this point. This was history in the making. *It's all going to be worth it!*

I was a senior in high school and now nearing the end of my K–12 education. I wouldn't say it had been easy. But, looking at the first president of the United States who looked like me, I felt my academic struggles would all be worth it in the end. I mean, surely, Barack Obama, a Black American man, had similar experiences in his education growing up as I had. Like me, I could imagine how he was often the only Black kid in his honors classes. I could imagine how, like me, he did not have a lot of racially affirming experiences in school. I could imagine how he, like me, dealt with prejudiced classmates at school, too, or had teachers who sometimes targeted him unfairly.

While standing in the cold, I reflected on my last few months in high school. I thought about how, during my senior spirit week, on Toga Day, when I decided to wear an American flag toga with the words "Yes We Can" and a picture of Barack Obama on it, the mocking chants of "NObama!" followed me down the hallway. I reflected on what it meant when my high school principal came over the intercom the day following the presidential election to reassure everyone there would be no "rioting" at his school. His announcement was in response to two White male students coming to school with "I hate niggers" written on their faces. They claimed they were protesting Black students arriving to school in suits, dress shirts, and ties to celebrate the historic event. I thought of how one of my White teachers was so infuriated by the 2008 election results that he practically refused to teach the entire next day. Or how at the same time as I was witnessing Barack Obama's exaltation to the pinnacle of Black American excellence, I also watched the low expectations White adults had for Black students play out in the classroom.

As I reflected, I thought: *Obama probably endured similar difficulties while in school, but he persevered, and now he is the president of the United States.* He represented—for all Americans, but especially Black students like myself—the hope of the American dream and the promise of our American public education system. If we strived hard to perform well, regardless of what was against us, and got good grades in the "best" classes, we could become president, too. *He is inspiring!* His inauguration was precisely what I needed to see. It was all going to be worth it in the end. Or so I thought.

Today, as I think back on that cold January day in 2009, and my conclusion that it would all be worth it, I question my rationale. Barack Obama being sworn in as president would prove to be simultaneously inspirational and devastating for me. Yes, it was a powerful symbol of progress in the fight for equity in this country and an affirmation of my personal struggle, and the fight of other Black kids like me. It led us to keep persisting. But more unexpectedly, it came to represent a powerful illusion that made me dig my heels in deeper to be successful in my circumstances and pardon the intentions of the American educational system that made it so hard to exist as a fully realized Black man. It was even more devastating to realize this was not only a powerful illusion for me but for millions of other students of color, too.

————

HIGH SCHOOL IS consistently sensationalized in American culture. I believe for many it is the high point of their educational journey and for a select few maybe even the high point of their lives. We often hear people reflect on the "glory days" of high school—reminiscing on their popularity, if they were recognized with superlatives, if they played sports or led cheers or held signs in the stands. Americans hold the high school experience in high esteem.

As a result, it is the educational experience that is most depicted in our media, its allure and agony inspiring countless sitcoms, teen movies, and hit songs.

Looking at the references to and illustrations of high school in our media can give insight into what we value as a society. More specifically, films show how Black and marginalized students are often portrayed and perceived as teenagers in the high school experience. Well-known movies like *Stand and Deliver* (1988), *Lean on Me* (1989), *Sister Act 2* (1993), *Menace II Society* (1993), *Dangerous Minds* (1995), and *Freedom Writers* (2007) use images of dangerous, violent, and criminalized students of color who are underperforming in school and need a teacher to save them. These students in the movies often come from broken homes and crime-ridden neighborhoods, and school is the last thing on their minds. The films project that school and the presence of a caring teacher is the only safe haven for these students and is what can deliver the teens from an otherwise doomed life.

One could argue that many of these movies are based on true stories or true events; therefore it is not the media that is perpetuating a narrative of Black and marginalized teens but rather just reflecting what is reality. Although I believe these depictions are somewhat exaggerated, I do agree that they are not fabricated and do reflect at least one reality that teens across the country live within. But I would also argue there are many other narratives that are playing out as well, that are not being told, and that do not get as much attention in our mainstream media. The hyperfocus on the Black or marginalized teen who is troubled and criminalized is what I am certain continues to seep into the minds of all Americans and perpetuates a mythical idea of Black youth, and more importantly impacts how our educators think about our high school students. Consistently media narratives that tell the same story have an impact in real life by shifting the expectations teachers have for certain students and how those students are then categorized before they even set foot in the classroom. These preconceived narratives certainly shaped my own high school experience.

AUGUST 18, 2005

Sumter High was like most other large high schools in the Southeast. Athletics were king. The athletes received the most attention from students and teachers. Friday night football games were a highlight for many in the city and especially for students. Our football and basketball teams had gone to the state championships numerous times. Coaches filled most of the male athletic teams with excellent Black athletes, athletes who made my six-foot, skinny stature at the time seem almost childlike in comparison.

On my first day of high school, I stood nervously in the Sumter High School cafeteria lunch line while two older Black girls, both about sixteen years old I figured, stood in front of me and exchanged life updates.

"Hey, girl! How was your summer? And congrats! How far along are you?" one of them said to the other.

"I'm five months!"

Wow, this is a wild introduction to high school, I thought, as I realized both of the young women were pregnant. They pulled out ultrasound pictures from their purses to admire their soon-to-be-born children. I was stunned. I was not surprised about high school pregnancy as that was pretty common in the Sumter I knew. But I was astonished that this conversation was the one I overheard on the first day of high school. I had entered a whole new universe.

While I was lost in my thoughts, what seemed like the entire Sumter High football team walked up behind me. I learned right then and there that, at Sumter High, the football players ate first, one of their many rewards for their competitive exceptionalism. As the players, mostly Black guys, stepped in front of me, I felt intimidated. A part of me still felt considerable anxiety and isolation every time popular Black male peers surrounded me. My insecurities were constantly bleeding out, and I imagined the football players were sharks that could smell blood in the water. It was like we all knew the script written for us and we mechanically assumed our roles. I couldn't break out of my role, and they couldn't break out of theirs. I think, at the deepest level, we all despised the entire performance.

That day was a Thursday, and on Thursdays, the "Country Kitchen" line served "world-famous" fried chicken and macaroni. I had even heard about how delicious this lunch was while in middle school. As I walked up to the lunch lady to receive my meal, she passed me a tray, but, in my nervousness, I dumped it right on my new camel-colored suede Adidas. *Damn.* Immediately, the football players started laughing.

One of them looked at me and said with a sneer, "You know you still have to pay for that, right? And they *aren't* giving you another one." He turned to his teammates and laughed some more. His snark prompted the two young women in front of me to come to my defense. They turned and said confidently, "Y'all leave him alone. You can tell he's a freshman, and this is his first day."

I could not have dreamed of a more embarrassing moment. In my attempt to show that I was unfazed, I retorted timidly, "No, I'm not paying for this! Ummm…I'll clean it up though." I thought I was about to be punished for dropping my food. The football players burst into laughter again.

Thankfully, the kind Black lunch lady looked at me and smiled. She said, "Here, sweetie," as she handed me another tray of fried chicken and macaroni. She continued, "Don't listen to them, you don't have to clean it up, and you don't have to pay for what you spilled."

I gripped my tray tightly and continued to walk through the line, head down. The football player who had antagonized me looked back as he left the lunch line, nodded his head at me, grinned, and said, "Stay up, young playa." I guess this was his way of apologizing.

In 1970—the year my father was born, and one year before my mother's birth, and sixteen years after the landmark *Brown v. Board of Education* ruling—Edmunds High School (the "White high school") and Lincoln High School (the "Black high school") in Sumter integrated to create Sumter High School. There were roughly 2,500 students enrolled, and the hallways were excessively crowded during class transitions. Like the rest of the schools within the district, Sumter High was almost evenly split between Black and White students. There was, in addition, a small population of Asian Americans.

The high school had been nicknamed "The Jailhouse" by many Black students because the layout of the school grounds resembled a prison. There was a significant amount of grassy land leading to the entrance with a guard at the front gate. There were even rumors that the school was initially built to be a prison but turned into a high school.

Students would frequently articulate how the environment felt prisonlike. Many administrators and school resource officers—school-based police officers—carried Tasers; there were strict hallway policies, many fights, and the occasional lunchroom "riot." I recall the first time I saw someone tased was at Sumter High during a fight between two students that a resource officer was struggling to break up. At the time, I did not feel strange about the environment or even necessarily unsafe because I assumed it was the norm.

As I learned on my first day, there was also a high rate of teenage pregnancy at Sumter High. So much so that the school provided a childcare center housed in a trailer behind the main building for those mothers who were attending classes while they raised children. It was common to see young mothers play with, feed, and care for their children during their lunch block.

Like in my previous school experiences, I distinguished myself as exceptional in a variety of ways at Sumter High. I had been playing the saxophone since middle school—receiving excellent ratings in state competitions and being awarded "first chair." So, as I entered high school, I wanted to keep playing the instrument I loved and excelled at. I continued as first chair in the band when I arrived at Sumter High. Further, I became the quintessential "involved" student through my freshman and sophomore years as a member of organizations like the Key Club, National Honor Society, and student government, in addition to band. If there was a club, I was a part of it. And my social life was going reasonably well, too. Most of my classes were filled with White students, many of the same students I knew in middle school. However, I also maintained friendships with my fellow Black classmates. I even dated a popular Black girl in my school. I was content and felt socially accepted by most of my peers.

However, like my earlier time in Sumter's school district, the majority of students in "high-achieving" classes were White. Living essentially in both worlds—the White student honors classes world, and the Black student world—presented an opportunity for me to be keenly aware of the differences in how high school was distinct for both of these groups. Little did I know at the start of high school how much more pronounced those differences would be once I entered the International Baccalaureate (IB) program at the beginning of my junior year.

When I entered the IB program, I was both excited and nervous. I knew that participating in such an advanced program would be challenging because of how difficult and time-consuming the courses were. However, I wanted to be a part of "the best" program because those affirmations validated me, and I believed that this course of study would provide me with the most advantageous future opportunities. Sumter High became affiliated with the IB program six years earlier, in 2001, and had its first graduating IB class from Sumter in the spring of 2004. IB was founded on principles of student-centered learning rather than the traditional teacher-centered, rote memorization learning that too often happens in American schools. The classes were interesting and allowed us to have discussions and critically debate topics, unlike the general education classes. There was space for us to be critical of our world and ask questions. The flexibility and autonomy afforded to the students in some of the program's curriculum were a more advanced version of my private preschool experience. Unsurprisingly, the IB program was comprised of mostly White students. Some of the students even transferred to participate in the IB curriculum from Wilson Hall, the town's all-White private school that was founded during the backlash to the *Brown v. Board of Education* school integration ruling in 1954.

There were only a few Black students and even fewer Black men in my IB program. The student demographics were somewhat diverse compared to the program's faculty, which was not racially diverse at all. Every teacher within the IB program was White. Even our IB Spanish teacher was a White woman originally from Spain. She would often joke about teaching us the "proper" or "correct" Spanish rather than what we learned from our Salvadoran Honors Spanish teacher in the ninth and tenth grades. Aside from being all-White, the teachers were also some of the most veteran educators. Many of them had been teaching for decades. One, in particular, had the privilege of teaching my mother, aunt, uncle, and myself. There was a sense of pride in these teachers. They were respected within the community and were asked by the administration to teach the IB students—the "best" students in the school.

We exceptional students had tremendous flexibility and privilege as well, privileges I began to realize were a reward only designed for those deemed "worthy" enough to receive them. However, the worthiness was not as "merit-based" as many claimed but rather a privilege granted to those fortunate enough to find themselves in these spaces—spaces that were fiercely exclusive, and protected by social norms and unspoken rules. It was highly difficult and unusual, for example, to move into an advanced class if you had not been tracked for honors courses earlier in your academic career. Although I became accustomed to these spaces and the privileges that came with them, existing in them remained a mental and emotional workout that caused cognitive dissonance within myself. Nevertheless, I was a high school student and enjoyed the advantages of being in the IB program. And like most high school students, my classmates and I would find ways to take advantage of those privileges as much as possible.

Honestly, looking back, I feel like my White female classmates in the IB program took the most advantage of the privileges we were granted. Two girls, in particular, would notoriously come to school late every morning because they "had to pick up breakfast from Chick-fil-A" and often brought their large, Styrofoam cups filled with sweet tea to our first-period class. Although it was a school-wide rule that students were not allowed to eat or drink in class, many of our IB teachers permitted this, "as long as it is not distracting from the lesson." Our ability to eat in class was in direct contrast to the multiple students I knew who were not in IB and had received referrals for the same activity. I yelped out in shock the first time I had a sip of the morning "sweet tea" the girls were drinking. Their supposedly innocent morning routine was actually a way to bring into school a concoction of 50 percent tea and 50 percent whiskey. I learned about the mix the hard way when they urged me to take a sip that promptly burned through my nostrils. That was my first taste of whiskey, and my outburst earned me a verbal reprimand for "being noisy" from my teacher. The two girls giggled. Aside from clandestinely drinking whiskey throughout the day, I noticed that many White girls in my classes were granted grace and favor in many other aspects. I believe this is when I fully understood how important the young White woman was in American culture and how there was practically an unconscious knee-jerk reaction to protect young White women and make them comfortable at all costs.

Interestingly enough, the advanced students all knew and accepted the lenient enforcement of rules for the young White women in class, and we would often use it to our advantage. In class with our White male IB teachers, we knew that if we wanted an assignment's deadline moved, we needed to have a White girl talk with the teacher on our behalf, and then our teachers would approve the request. This intersection of the creepy "White male gaze" and the privilege of young White women created the perfect scenario for us in those moments.

Although young White women had particular advantages in our IB program, we all did in one way or another. IB students had a different bell schedule from the rest of the school. Our classes were longer, so we changed them less frequently and at off times. We had a pink-colored sticker on our student IDs that allowed us to be in the hallway at any time we wanted. The sticker helped the resource officers and administrators know that we were IB kids and had a "right" to be in the hallway. We would often use our pink stickers to walk around the halls without reason, even if we were supposed to be in class. Also, that sticker came in handy when we would leave campus early. All we had to do was show the guards at the gate our sticker that indicated we were IB students and mention we had an "offsite project" or "test" and they would allow us to leave campus without being signed out by a parent or guardian. I, along with my classmates, occasionally left campus midday to have lunch downtown for multiple hours and then come back without anyone batting an eye.

This special treatment built a sense of being above the rules, almost like the athletes in the school. We were the "good kids," so everyone turned a blind eye to our collective mischievous behaviors. Although other Black students in the program and I benefited from some of the privileges we all received, we understood that these privileges were unique to the space.

However, our White counterparts, we soon learned, were experiencing these privileges in every other aspect of their lives. My White male classmates would often tell me stories about their weekend adventures that would infuriate me. My friend David mentioned how police stopped him and some of his other friends when he was driving home under the influence of alcohol and, instead of arresting him, the officer called his parents and let him off with a slap on the wrist. Or, in other instances, police officers would get calls to break up bonfires happening on my classmates' private property, and even if they would find alcohol or the occasional drugs on the premises, everyone merely received warnings or slaps on the wrists. I would argue with them that the reason they received grace was because they were White. They would rebut and say it all wasn't a big deal and that the cops knew they were "good kids" and "meant well." Their responses enraged me more and more. A part of me, though, knew they would never understand. They did not grow up with an incarcerated father, they had not experienced their family members or friends getting arrested or harassed for minor infractions. They were always protected by society and often never had to face hard consequences for their actions. Their

Whiteness was an ever-present shelter. It was a tough pill to swallow but one that I had swallowed long ago. When it came down to it, although we all received privileges, I was still a Black student in my IB program, and a Black citizen of Sumter, South Carolina. No pink sticker could entirely change the experience of being young and Black in America.

In more recent headlines, selective programs and advanced classes in high schools have been used as clickbait and the debate surrounding them has become increasingly polarized. The United States Office of Civil Rights has released data revealing how racially segregated selective programs are within our nation's high schools. There have been many calls for action to change these statistics and to include all students in advanced courses. Further, there has been much conversation on the curriculum in these selective programs as well.

The debate over critical race theory (CRT) has seized the media's attention and has become highly politicized. In my opinion, the attack on CRT is a full and outright attack on our education system.

In 2023, the College Board, a national nonprofit that develops AP courses for high schools, made the decision to revise their AP African American Studies course, removing many of the topics that were being scrutinized by conservative critics. Some critics, such as Governor Ron DeSantis of Florida, went as far as banning the course altogether in high schools across his state. Many social justice organizations and leaders across the country took significant issue with the College Board's choice to amend the curriculum to appease critics, and some even called it educational malpractice. The highly critical lens and biased targeting that curriculum which highlights Black liberatory movements undergoes has divided Americans perhaps more than any educational controversy since school desegregation, as have stories of Black excellence, and attempts to tell the true extent of historical, racial atrocities in this country. But even before the conversation around the teaching of racial histories in advanced high school courses became mainstream, I would argue that marginalized students were already falling victim to an erasure of their histories, unfair targeting, and outright denial of their humanity in advanced classes. This was certainly my experience.

WHEN I WALKED into my AP US History class, a required course for all IB students, I noticed that my White male teacher, Dr. Shuler, had placed a news article on my desk. I looked at him and saw he wore a sly smirk—an expression that was familiar to me and signaled that this class period was going to be a long one. As I sat down and the remainder of the students settled in, I heard Dr. Shuler say, "Brian, did you read the news article on your desk? I thought it was very interesting."

I looked down and read the headline which stated that Black men have a lower life expectancy than any other demographic in the United States. In my opinion, Dr. Shuler relished talking about Black people in disparaging ways. My belief was confirmed by how he spoke about his "maid," an illiterate Black woman. He told us how his wife, out of the "kindness" of her heart, taught her how to read ("free of charge!"). He even loved to tell us how he bought his "maid" gifts of "whiskey" for the holidays so she and her boyfriend could have a "good time." He reduced her to a caricature, to a punchline in his offensive jokes.

As I silently read the title of the article on my desk, he continued, "So, what are your thoughts?"

Now the entire class was staring at me, including him. I was annoyed. *Why is he trying to start something with me today? Can't I just sit in class in peace?* I paused for a moment to collect myself, and with a confused look on my face, I said, "Why did you put this on my desk?"

He then said, "I thought it would be something that would interest you because it's a shame that Black men have such a short life expectancy. You don't think that's interesting?"

I responded, "No, not really, because I am going to live a long time, and so are the Black men in my family."

The class was now looking with expressions on their faces that can only be summed up as *WTF?* Dr. Shuler always liked to push his students' buttons, but this was even extreme for him. My friend and classmate, a White male named Peter, said, "That's a strange thing to put on Brian's desk, Dr. Shuler," to which my teacher replied, "I don't know. When I saw that, I was like man, y'all [Black men] should get a discounted rate on your Social Security or something since you don't live that long," and he began to laugh. I did not find any of it funny and mocked his laugh as I asked if we could please move on.

Unfortunately, Dr. Shuler was not the only teacher I experienced these tense interactions with. My IB science teacher, Mr. Smith, practically became my archnemesis while I was in his class. He was a conservative White man who was highly opinionated. At the time, Barack Obama was the presidential hopeful, and Mr. Smith would offer unsolicited and unwarranted rants about how we were all "doomed" if this "Muslim" Black man became our president. He would go on to say how he was already buying "rounds of ammo" and other weapons to prepare when the government tried to strip him of his Second Amendment right to bear arms if Barack Obama won the White House. Mr. Smith would also refer to the future president as the next Adolf Hitler with statements like "everyone loved Hitler in the beginning, too." I thought he was one of the most abrasive and ignorant people I had ever met and could not believe he was my IB science teacher. I often would state that he "should not talk about politics with his students."

Our regular disagreements, many of which I felt were against this racialized backdrop, all came to a head one day in class over an argument regarding my cell phone. In Mr. Smith's class, there was a rule that we could not use cell phones. However, because we were IB students and seen as "mature," he told us that any rule we had to follow in his class, he would follow as well. One day I received a text from my mother while in class, so I quickly checked, responded, and then put my phone away.

Mr. Smith saw me and said, "Give me your phone."

I knew I had broken a rule and replied, "Oh, I'm sorry, I was just responding to something quickly. I will put it up now, and you won't see it again." That answer did not satisfy him as he further asked why I thought it was acceptable to break the rules.

I mentioned that I had received a text from my mother, and I quickly responded while we were working silently. My words gave him the ammunition he needed as he answered back, "Oh, so your mother promotes that you break the rules, huh? That explains a lot."

His words astonished me. *He doesn't even know my mother, so why is he saying anything about her?* I felt like he was needlessly provoking me. The intensity quickly escalated over what I knew was a small incident. I replied, "You don't even know my mother, so please don't say anything about her. Let's change the topic, please." I was desperately trying to have him get off this subject because it was making my blood boil. I was glaring at him without blinking, trying to burn a hole in his face with my eyes. In my mind, I had already made peace with going to jail for assault.

Mr. Smith continued, "Well, I know her well enough to know that she texts you during class, which is clearly against the rules, so I know she encourages bad behavior."

I was livid. I responded, "Well, you should take your own advice. You were just using your cell phone moments before I used mine." So, with that, thankfully we dropped it.

Later that evening, at home, I told my mother and grandmother what had happened. My grandma Clara scolded me. She said I should know better than to "take the bait" and that "those teachers want you to get kicked out of school, and you're falling right into the trap." She went on to say they were "hateful White men." I imagine this was triggering and scary for her. She was from a different generation, and she knew how horrible the consequences of challenging White authority figures could be. When my grandmother was thirteen, White male doctors refused to help her and her siblings carry their father into the hospital after he suffered a massive heart attack in Clarendon County, South Carolina. The White doctors and nurses only watched as the children struggled. My grandmother often reflects on how her father died in her arms in her attempt to get him up the hospital ramp while the White adults around her watched. So, for her, indeed, some White men were truly hateful. I understood her perspective, but I did not regret how I handled things at my school. However, I promised my mother and grandmother that moving forward, I would follow the class rules and ignore any comments meant to upset me.

Besides the constant bullying from two of my White male teachers, there was also an unspoken way of life in our classes within IB. Similar to my White girl classmates' privileges, my White boy classmates, especially my friend David, were seen as model students, and teachers primarily focused on them. David was highly competitive and truly smart. He would often ask classmates what grade they made on assignments simply to confirm that he did better. My teachers loved him. In my mind, he was the archetypal young White male. He was athletic, he was brilliant, and a "good ol' boy." My White male teachers saw a younger version of themselves in David and my White female teachers looked at him as their son. He could do no wrong, it seemed. Many of my teachers, especially the White women, would specifically teach to David. If David understood the lecture, then misunderstandings from other students were irrelevant—especially the Black students. Often when my fellow Black classmates or I would ask for help during class, my teachers would get irritated and reply, "This is slowing down the lesson." It became so problematic that I would ask David to pretend he did not understand a lesson to get the teachers to reteach or slow down a bit. It was a way of life that we accepted and learned to navigate.

Looking back, I often wonder if I should have spoken up more about what I noticed in the disparaging behaviors of my teachers. How would they have responded? I believe these experiences catalyzed a substantial shift within me during high school, a time when I was becoming more accustomed to my White environment's unspoken ways of life. The change was not only happening to me but to all other students around me. Systems and cultures have an uncanny way of grinding you into submission, forcing you to submit to their power, making you hate every moment that you choose not to give in. Yes, I stood up for myself often. But not to the point that I would be unsuccessful in the system. Accomplishing the goal of high achievement was my most important task at hand. I needed to be successful in the system, and I would do that by any means possible.

I BELIEVE THAT one of the unspoken consequences of exceptionalism in school is that those historically marginalized students who embody what it means to be the so-called exception carry a heavy weight on their shoulders. These students in some ways have bought into the falsehood that they are exceptional, that they are not like the rest of the people who look like them or come from their same background, and because they are different, they must maintain their status to be accepted in the broader mainstream society and to be resurrected from a social death.

While the students feel this pressure and isolation, often those around them that are on the other side of the coin—those who are *not* achieving or who are *not* deemed as exceptional—become resentful of those who are. This resentment leads to further separation between the two groups and continues a vicious cycle, a cycle that furthers the inherent mission of the White supremacist system, allowing it to persist.

VISITATIONS HAD ONCE again become more frequent with my father. He had moved from a federal correctional institution in Petersburg, VA, to one in Williamsburg, SC, only an hour away from Sumter. I visited him weekly. I could not hang out with friends during my weekends or do other teenage activities like a typical high school student. Instead, my weekends consisted of working until the Chick-fil-A store closed on Friday night and Saturday, then visiting my father in prison from 8:00 A.M. to 3:00 P.M. on Sunday. After Sunday visits, I would get home, eat, and then work on assignments that I needed to complete for my IB courses. On the occasional Saturday that I did not work, I would visit my father. It was almost as if I lived a double life; none of my friends in high school knew about my father's incarceration. They only knew my mom and I lived with my grandparents and that I never mentioned my father.

Our prison visits generally were pleasant; I was usually tired because I had arrived home late from closing at Chick-fil-A the night before only to get up early on Sunday morning to maximize the visitation time. Also, I looked forward to eating the food from the visitation room vending machines, but we had to be there early to get first dibs. My family liked the hot wings, cheese-cake slices, and fruit snacks. Not your ideal breakfast food, but it did the trick.

Although visits were typically positive, there were underlying tensions that were snowballing between my father and me. By the end of my junior year, my mother was unemployed. The market crash of 2008 impacted every American, and my mother was no exception. She had lost her job working for Nationwide Insurance because they were downsizing. Luckily, we were living with my grandparents, so finances were manageable. But resources were tight. At the same time, my father had found himself in trouble with fellow inmates because he owed them money. His debts were a stark contrast from the previous year, where family members of his fellow inmates would meet my mother and me in the parking lot and give us one hundred dollars here or two hundred and fifty dollars there to settle debts their inmate owed my father. We never really asked what he was doing, but we were happy for the money. Now, though, the tables had turned. He was in some sort of "big trouble" and needed a constant flow of money sent to his "books" to pay back his debts to survive.

My mother always had a place in her heart for my father. I believe this stemmed from the deep ancestral drive Black women often feel to protect Black men. I have witnessed this drive many times throughout my lifetime. Also, I imagine my mother held my father in her heart because he gave her me—her only child. So, she would often send him money each time he would ask. My father's money requests were slowly making me angrier and angrier because my mother was unemployed, and I was a high school student going into my senior year, so expenses were coming up. My frustration finally came to a climax one Sunday while in the visitation room. My mother had just sent money to my father, and I told her in our car ride to the prison that she should not send him any more money. I told her that it was selfish of him to continue to ask for money when he knew that his son and wife were struggling. My mother listened to me but she did not think I would share these same thoughts with my father.

Once in the visitation room, I started to express my sentiments. I told my father that finances were tight and asking for fifty or one hundred dollars often hurt us. I went on to say that I just didn't think gambling in prison was smart, and that he should rethink his actions. My father became noticeably irritated as I mentioned this to him. He was staring at me with rage in his eyes as if I had committed the ultimate betrayal.

With a low tone of calmness in his voice, with an undertone of rage, he asked, "Brian, how old are you?"

I responded, "Seventeen."

He then said, "How old am I?"

I answered, "Thirty-eight."

He replied, "So if you only lived seventeen years of life and I have lived thirty-eight... how the fuck do you think you can tell me what to do?" His words sent a spark through my bones.

I had thought I'd let go of all my negative feelings toward my father, but at this moment, I realized I had only suppressed them. I was on fire with anger after he spoke to me that way, with disdain and condescension. My eyes stretched, and I said with a loud, strong stream-of-consciousness outburst, "I'm a senior in high school, and I have plenty of things that I need my mom to help me pay for, but I know she is not working, so I don't ask her, and I sacrifice! I work, and I save money that I should be spending to have fun with my friends but instead, I save up because I know my mother can't afford to do the things that need to happen! A seventeen-year-old does that! But you instead gamble, in prison of all places, have people threatening your life, or at least you're pretending that they are so my unemployed mother can constantly send you money while she and your son struggle! A seventeen-year-old sacrifices while a thirty-eight-year-old acts immature and selfish!" As I got my last words out, my father stood up and lunged at me. My mother jumped up with tears in her eyes to block me, and I stood up and walked quickly to the exit door. I was not about to fight my father, especially not in a federal prison visitation room.

The correctional officers eyed my father from across the room, and one even started to walk in our direction. They were ready to subdue him—and me—if they had to. I continued to walk in the direction of the exit door. Once I arrived, I stood by the door shaking from adrenaline and anger. We were only allowed to leave at certain times, but I was going to wait by that door for hours if I had to because, in my mind, I was never talking to my father again. My mother was crying and hugged my father goodbye. I imagine this hug was partially out of fear and partially out of sadness. My father called for me to come to hug him, and I ignored him. Everyone in the visitation room was now looking at us and whispering. We were the new gossip for the visitors this Sunday afternoon. But I did not care at all. My mother then walked toward me and waited by the door as well, and the guards went to walk my father back to his living quarters. I stood by the door silently and enraged. I refused to say a word to my mother.

I was never coming back.

———

"Sup, bro? How have you been?" my classmate asked me as we were waiting in the gymnasium during an assembly for seniors.

I responded, "I've been good. How about you? Looking forward to being out of here, finally?"

The classmate was a Black male acquaintance that I used to be closer with at the beginning of high school but lost touch with as I transitioned into the IB program. We remained cordial and friendly anytime we saw each other.

My friend then stated, "Yeah, man, I'm looking forward to graduating, and I'm trying to go to NYU. I'm ready to get out of Sumter, ya know?"

It seemed like every Black person's dream was to one day "get out of Sumter." I agreed with his sentiments and was excited to hear he applied to NYU. Emory University was my top choice, but I was interested in New York University as well.

I excitedly said, "Oh man, that's great. I know those application essays were a beast. How do you feel about your application?"

He looked at me with a blank stare. "Oh nah, man, I haven't applied yet."

I thought: *It's January. I'm pretty sure the application deadline has passed!* I tried to give him the benefit of the doubt; maybe the application was due in the next few days. I knew that NYU was one of the few schools that required an SAT 2 test or a subject SAT test. To quickly change the subject, I said, "Oh, gotcha; well, which subject SAT did you take?" My friend stared at me with confusion, as if he didn't know what the subject SAT was, and then went on to say that he had not taken the SAT yet.

Now I knew that he had no clue about the requirements to apply to NYU and possibly any other school he was interested in. Had his guidance counselor not said anything to him about it? My IB guidance counselor spoke with us religiously about college applications and had even given me nine application fee waivers to cover the cost of my fees because she knew my mother was unemployed. She was intimately involved in helping the IB students through their college application process. Then I realized his counselor probably did not help him at all.

I asked, "Hey man, do you know who your guidance counselor is? They should be able to help with your application to NYU or whatever school you're thinking about."

He then informed me that he had only talked to his counselor once throughout his entire time at Sumter High, and she was not very interested in helping him. I think he could tell by my facial expression that it was nearly impossible for him to get into NYU this year. He just stared at me. I stared back. We both knew that his counselor had failed him.

After a brief but palpable silence, he broke by saying, "All right bruh, it was good talking to you. Good luck with everything. Keep killin' it, man!"

I responded, "Same to you, man. Good luck with everything!" And we walked away from each other into different futures.

————————

AT THE END of my senior year in high school, I was celebrated for a service project that I led as a requirement for my IB program. As a part of the curriculum, each student had to participate in CAS, which stood for Creativity, Action, and Service. CAS was my favorite part of the IB program because it allowed us to be creative, innovative, and service oriented. For my CAS project, I decided to develop a mentorship program for children living in a local children's home in Sumter. My classmates and I would visit the home biweekly to conduct programming and tutor the kids.

Interestingly enough, as I designed and led the mentorship program, I never once mentioned to anyone that I had an incarcerated parent. Many of those kids had similar experiences, but I never dared to share mine with them. I now understand how powerful it would have been for those children, especially those who had incarcerated parents, to know that I shared in their experience. Instead, I chose to allow my ultimate family secret to remain private in fear that my worth would decrease immensely in the eyes of my friends, teachers, and everyone else. Once they knew about my father's transgressions, I feared my status as exceptional would be diminished. Also, I wanted to protect my father, who the world had consistently said was not exceptional. I had been in these "elite" spaces with these people, and I knew how brutal they could be. I tried to protect him from this part of society's judgments and criticisms. Subconsciously, an element of me was still deeply connected to my father, and inexplicably I felt responsible for his actions. I feared others' judgment of him, my mother, myself, and my family.

Regardless of my lack of vulnerability, the program was remarkably successful. And at the end of the year, the director wanted to gift my fellow mentors and me with a token of appreciation for our contributions. She gave me Dr. Seuss's book *Oh, the Places You'll Go!* with signatures from all the children we had worked with. As the director read the book aloud, I was reminded of my own dreams. I hoped to go to the farthest of places, "move mountains!" and realize my greatest ambitions. I had also hoped that everything I had endured until this point would be worthwhile. I reflected on her gift and her words and thought about the children. Would they have bright futures, too? What would happen to them? Was our presence there truly impactful? As of 2018, roughly 31 percent of children living in alternative situations graduate from high school. And of that 31 percent a majority of them remain impoverished throughout their adult lives. So, honestly, what heights will those children reach, and what places will they go?

Kurt Vonnegut once said, "High school is closer to the core of the American experience than anything else I can think of." These words resonate with me. I would go on further to say that not only is high school the educational period closest to the core of the American experience, but it is also the embodiment of the unspoken values at the core of America. I believe we are exposed to these values little by little throughout our educational process, in the same way we learn to swim with floaties to get comfortable with the water and the bittersweet taste of chlorine. However, high school pushes us into the deep end without goggles, and the chlorine burns our eyes until we get adjusted. Once adjusted, we either assume our roles and accept the world for what it is, or we reject them and drown.

Our American values are seen in high school through the idolization and praise of Black athletes for their physical abilities while little to no emphasis is placed on their intellectual or emotional capacity. Our American values can be seen in the criminalization of high school students, primarily Black and Brown, that reinforces the American-held belief in their delinquent nature. Our American values can be seen in the systematic separation and social privileges given to those who are "high achieving," often the most wealthy and White students. Our American values can be seen in the emphasis placed on following expectations rather than challenging them, learning and redeploying existing ideas rather than being encouraged to originate them, and accepting the status quo. Public high school in America is a social microcosm and reveals key beliefs that we hold dear as a country. Therefore, it is no surprise that high school dropouts carry out 75 percent of all the crimes committed in America. And that those most likely to drop out of high school are Black and Brown students. By the time we arrive in ninth grade and especially as we begin to experience high school, we understand where we fall within the societal hierarchy, and a rejection of that hierarchy is a rejection of living freely within our society as we know it.

So, the question to pose is: What would happen if we did things differently? What if high school empowered students, encouraged civic engagement, truly affirmed racial, cultural, sexual, gender, and religious identities? What if we fostered original ideas, supported critical thinking, challenged societal norms, and provided tools and resources for students to chart their own paths? What if high school was the last stop on a liberatory educational journey that freed us all from the script and embedded caste system that society has given us? What would that mean for our educational system? What would it mean for our nation?

As I reflect on these questions and on my high school experience, I think about how much I, a young, intellectual Black man who wasn't afraid to speak his mind, upset those in authority. I also think about what could have happened if I did not have the protection and privilege of being an exceptional student in my school's IB program. I can make assumptions based on personal familiarity and statistics. My father, my uncles, and one of my cousins all had their first experience with the criminal justice system in high school. My sixth-grade best friends Carlos and Alain did, too.

I consider high school a time where all students begin to internalize where they will end up in life—they think of those "places they will go," those "heights they will reach." It is in high school, I believe, where we begin to perceive and internalize our official place in society and who we can become as adults. We begin to ask the questions, What places can we actually reach in our lives? What does the future hold for us? And the replies to those questions are reflected back to us vividly. For those Black and historically marginalized teens the answers are often bleak. Therefore, if we want to change the response that many students often receive, it is time that we revolutionize the way we think about our education system and our high schools. It is time for us to create secondary schools that prepare students for the changing world, and give them knowledge, experiences, and skills necessary to thrive. It is time for us to right an inherent wrong in our education system and treat all students like full human beings in our structures and curriculum. It is time for us to do something radically different. If we don't, I'm afraid to see what places our education system will go, and what lows we will reach.

PART III

Postsecondary Education: College and Career

CHAPTER 6

Just Another Case of Affirmative Action

It is not our differences which separate [us] but our reluc-
tance to recognize those differences.

— AUDRE LORDE, 1984

S ENDING A CHILD TO COLLEGE is practically synonymous with
the white-picket-fence, nuclear-family fantasy many Americans hold dear. Though the perceived value of a college education
is currently in flux, I still believe the majority of American parents
hope their children will further their education beyond a high
school diploma even if they themselves did not receive a college
degree. This was the dream my grandparents had for my parents
and my parents had for me even if it went, at times, unspoken. Because this aspiration is so widespread in our society, the majority
of Americans strive for college attendance in some way. As of 2018,
over 60 percent of American adults aged twenty-five and older reported that they had attended some college. However, only about
42 percent of Americans age twenty-five and older successfully
obtain some sort of college degree.

Like all other aspects of our American educational system, sta-
tistically speaking, college attendance, college success, and,
ultimately, college graduation are substantially connected to a per-

son's race. According to the US Department of Education, as of 2021, only 15 percent of all full-time college students enrolled were Black. Though that number is low, what is more concerning is the wide racial gap in college graduation rates. As of 2022, 68 percent of white students graduate within six years while the percentage of Black students graduating within six years is significantly lower, registering at about 45 percent. This graduation gap between White students and Black students is even wider at highly selective and elite private colleges and universities.

Many scholars and authors have begun to write about the challenges that Black and other marginalized students face in colleges, especially in predominantly White, elite institutions. Notably, Anthony Abraham Jack writes about this phenomenon extensively in his 2019 book *The Privileged Poor: How Elite Colleges Are Failing Disadvantaged Students*. In his work, he outlines the challenges poor students face in these environments, challenges that often extend beyond the academic sphere.

What my time attending an institution of higher education and now working for one has shown me is that college only continues to replicate the undercurrent of racial and social hierarchy our public K–12 system establishes. The commonly held myths of exceptionalism, meritocracy, and color blindness may even, I would argue, be *more* prevalent in higher education spaces. The belief in these dangerous myths is ever-present and unfortunately was encoded on June 29, 2023, in the Supreme Court's decision to overturn decades of precedent supporting race-conscious admission programs used across America in colleges and universities. The six-justice conservative supermajority within the Supreme Court invalidated these admissions programs with its historic decision to repeal what is more commonly known as affirmative action.

It's sickening, yet not surprising, to realize that in 2023, we as a society are still grappling with the fallacy that Black and Brown students are receiving admissions to a college education undeservingly. That is what this decision truly says. The harsh Supreme Court decision argues for a colorblind or race-blind approach to college admissions because that approach creates "fairness" and removes "shortcuts" for Black and Brown students. However, people who argue this position fail to realize or properly understand that every other aspect of the lived educational experience of young Americans leading up to the point of college admissions is dramatically unequal and the opposite of colorblind. Justice Ketanji Brown Jackson poignantly summed up this point in her dissent when she wrote, "deeming race irrelevant in law does not make it so in life." As I have discussed throughout this book, the American way of educating children has everything to do with their color, with their race—from the resources afforded to the schools they attend, to their educational opportunities in the classroom, to how their teachers interact with them, to the quality of their teachers, to what they are being taught, to how they are disciplined, and so much more. Therefore, any opportunity to right the wrongs of the previous thirteen years of a student's educational experience and ensure more racial diversity on our college campuses should be welcomed, not fought against.

I shudder at what this decision will mean for college campuses across the country. History has already shown us: the nineteen states that banned race-conscious admissions in their public colleges and universities ("state schools") prior to the recent Supreme Court decision had a significant decline in the number of Black, Latino, and Native American students attending those institutions. Now, this trend will surely continue in all of the higher education institutions both public and private across the nation.

The ongoing rhetoric and paradigm that eventually led to the decision to overturn affirmative action programs has long been looming on American college campuses since those same campuses began to integrate. And attempting to navigate through this underbelly as a marginalized student can be extremely strenuous.

AUGUST 15, 2009

When I started as a first-year student at Emory University, I was on cloud nine. Through a series of outside scholarships, a federal Pell Grant, and Emory's generous need-based financial aid package—which factored in my mother's unemployment—I paid nothing for my first year of college.

Emory was not my initial first-choice school. I had a clear vision: to move out of Sumter and go to college in a "big city." But my dreams of moving to Chicago were shot down when my mother expressed that my first-choice school, the University of Chicago, was not a viable application choice because I had no family there. In an emergency, she reasoned, she would not be able to afford the flights from the East Coast to Chicago. However, she did drive me south to visit the Atlanta campus of Emory University during my senior year of high school. That's when I fell in love with the college. The tour guide was extremely welcoming and friendly. The campus was beautiful. The white marble buildings twinkled in the sunlight, the quad was filled with smiling students, and the welcoming tone of every student we spoke with was noticeable. So, after I visited Emory, I was happy to make the well-regarded Atlanta school my top choice.

Founded in 1836, Emory University is a prestigious private research institution sometimes referred to as the "Harvard of the South." It has one of the largest university endowments among US universities and colleges at $11 billion, thanks in large part to its connections with the Coca-Cola Company. When I applied, Emory was ranked as the seventeenth-best university and college by *US News and World Report*. Because of its reputation and rankings, Emory attracted students from all over the country and world. There were students from all fifty states and fifty-seven countries in my incoming admitted class. I was one of about five hundred Black students admitted that year and, as such, I made up one small part of the approximately 7 percent of admitted students who were Black. The diversity in the student population was a stark contrast to what I was used to in Sumter. I was excited to broaden my horizons and meet individuals I had not come across before. For instance, my first-year roommate was a second-generation Indian American student. As I chatted with him online and by phone in the weeks leading up to our move-in, I wanted to learn more about his experience, country of origin, and everything in between. My roommate was a prime example of why I wanted to attend a school like Emory—to expand my worldview and meet people that I would be less likely to cross paths with in South Carolina.

Once I arrived at Emory, a massive part of my initial experience was the saturation of Black students, Black events, and the emphasis on a collective "Black Emory" community. This caught me off guard. I had been around Black people all my life, I always felt comfortable in my Blackness, and I understood the challenges and strategic tactics needed to move successfully as a Black person through a White world. However, I had never seen so much emphasis by students on creating a thriving Black community in an educational setting. I felt like I immediately had a group of friends and people who genuinely cared about my social, academic, and emotional well-being.

This community was comforting at first. Because the Black student community was small at Emory, there was an emphasis placed on creating a safe space for incoming students to feel welcomed. As I began to get to know many of my newfound friends, one of the things I noticed was, though we were all Black and shared some cultural similarities, there were significant differences between my experience and the collective. This realization brought meaning to the phrase "Black people are not a monolith."

Most of the Black students I encountered at Emory were children of immigrants—meaning their parents had immigrated to America from countries such as Nigeria, Haiti, Jamaica, Ghana, and those of the Caribbean islands. Black immigrants often represent a significant portion of the Black population in these elite spaces. Growing up in South Carolina, I had not met any Black immigrant families. Most Black people around me had a long history of living in South Carolina that could often be traced back to a legacy of racialized experiences in America. Aside from the children of Black immigrants, most of the other Black Emory students who I called "Black American" came from families in a completely different socioeconomic category than mine. Their parents, and sometimes grandparents, were doctors, lawyers, or well-off businesspeople.

These differences began to create a strange alienation within the Emory subculture I felt most comfortable in. My grandparents would often try to send me additional money to counter my feelings of isolation because of my financial background. My grandmother Clara went as far as significantly diminishing her savings to give me money so I could take part in a spring break trip that my friends were planning. In addition to my perception of the financial disparities, I also never came across anyone who had an incarcerated parent or even incarcerated family members, for that matter. Or at least they never shared that information with me. I would often allude to experiences of having an incarcerated parent to test the waters without giving myself away to my friends. I was searching for anyone who had a common experience. But I was often met with responses that showed either a completely negative judgment for those incarcerated or a complete unawareness of that lived reality. Because of these discouraging responses, I concluded that Emory was not a safe space to share the truth of my experience. Though Black students surrounded me within this faction of the Emory community, I felt different from them, and I was unsure what to make of it.

Despite feelings of separation, I became highly involved in campus activities during my first semester. I ran to be the president of my freshman dorm and, through determined campaigning, I won. Being the president of my residence hall was a fantastic way to meet other students and expand my social network. Also, I decided to run to be the freshman class representative in Emory's Student Government Association (SGA). In the second semester of my freshman year, I was elected to the SGA as one of three class representatives.

I was thrilled. I felt like I could thrive in Emory's environment in many more ways than in my high school. Initially, to me, college represented everything right with the education system. In my mind, I was living out the American dream. The school was diverse, the environment was welcoming, and the courses were delightfully rigorous. And for me, most importantly, I was not experiencing overtly racist behaviors in the ways I had experienced in Sumter.

Well, at least not yet.

———

As I HAVE highlighted throughout the previous chapters, implicit bias plays a major role in how marginalized students move through our education system. This is no different in higher education. Similar to the national trend in K–12 education, roughly 65 percent of educators in higher education are White, a disproportionate number when compared to the college student population: approximately 51 percent of students on campuses are White.

Further, according to a study published in the *Journal of Diversity in Higher Education*, White faculty members believed that they were "treating minority students no differently than they were treating their White students, but at the same time they held contradictory beliefs such as minority students being academically inferior or unprepared." These professors would use "colorblind language to describe their students as academically inferior, less prepared and less interested in pursuing graduate studies," the study found.

Inequitable policies, structures, and cultural norms already established at these universities play significantly into students' ability to succeed. What's worse, as I came to realize in my own experience, is that those who believe most strongly in these structures within the universities, often professors, can cause the most damage.

———

WHEN I LOOKED down at my paper, I saw a "D-" written in red ink accompanied by a note: "Brian, you must go to the writing center before turning in future papers."

I was shocked. I could wrap my head around receiving any other grade on a paper other than an almost failing grade. And then to be given an imperative that I must receive writing coaching from Emory's writing center before turning in future papers? I was startled.

This negative response to my writing, from a White woman graduate student in the sociology department, was in complete contrast to what I had previously received in my other courses that focused on writing. In my freshman writing seminar, a renowned and tenured Emory professor had praised my writing ability. After our first writing assignment, she even announced to the class that I was the only student who earned an A on the paper. So, getting this letter grade and being told to get help from the writing center in my sophomore year seemed unusual, even suspicious.

Further, the only other people who received the same feedback were my other Black friends in the class. The professor essentially told each Black student that they needed to visit the writing center before turning in future papers. I could not vouch for my classmates' writing ability, but I knew my own. And I knew that this paper was not as bad as she claimed.

This episode was new for me. I certainly experienced biased teachers throughout my K–12 education, but their biases never impacted how they graded my work. There was an objective grading process and code of conduct that, regardless of how any teacher may have felt about me, they followed. If I performed well academically, they did not undermine that. Even my highly problematic high school AP history teacher, Dr. Shuler, submitted my history essay to a citywide writing competition that I won.

Therefore, the subjectivity that I was experiencing with my college grades was shocking and, honestly, in the moment, felt more damaging than any negative comments or actions my previous educators had said or done. My professor's behavior felt dangerous and could affect how I matriculated through Emory. I was insulted. I had already decided that I was not going to the writing center for further coaching regardless of the professor's request. To be clear: Emory University's student-led writing center was an excellent resource for students. I had friends who worked for the writing center, and I valued their work. However, mainly White students staffed the center. Candidly, I only ever knew and heard of White students hired by the center at the time. It seemed to me that my professor assumed that the few Black students in her class needed writing support in ways that White students at Emory did not.

When the time came to turn in our next paper, instead of going to the writing center as requested by my professor, I lied and indicated a false day and time that I received writing support. I wanted to see if my suspicions were correct about her bias. I wrote this assignment in the same style as my first assignment, and I used the same writing method to argue my point. Remarkably when the paper was returned, the professor had given me a B+ with a note, "Brian, this essay is such an improvement. I am glad you went to the writing center. They really helped you get clearer in your writing! :)." After her thoughtless response, my professor's opinion became irrelevant to me. Instead of telling her what I did, I continued to falsely indicate writing support prior to turning in my papers, and she continued to praise how the center's coaching was "improving my writing ability." It began to dawn on me: maybe Emory was not the perfect school after all.

I put that experience behind me and continued to push forward in my classes. But there was another class that I struggled with in my sophomore year. This science course was required for psychology majors at Emory and had a reputation for being one of the more challenging courses at the university.

At the end of the semester, I made a C, and decided to retake the course with a different professor to potentially earn a better grade. I thought this was a smart move because, at the time, I planned to get a graduate degree in psychology.

The following semester, I went to the only other professor in the department who taught the course, a White male tenured professor, and I told him I wanted to retake the course. I asked if it was okay for me to do so with him though I technically already had the requirement completed. He obliged, and I enrolled in his class. My semester in his class was more or less uneventful. I noticed that the professor seemed uninterested in talking with me or building a relationship. However, his behavior was normal for a lot of professors in the science departments with all students. Many of them were researchers first and professors second. The disconnection and coldness from him was noticeable but not enough to upset me. As the semester ended, I eagerly waited for my final grade because I knew I had done better than my previous methods class, and I was excited about my improvement.

On a summer day, while I was at my work-study job at the Emory Autism Center, I received an email that final grades were ready for student viewing. I was impatient to see how I did in my psych course. As I logged into the student portal to review my transcript, I noticed that an "I" was posted as a fill-in for the letter grade. I did not know what "I" meant and immediately thought it was a mistake. I emailed my professor to tell him about the transcript's error and ask for my final grade. He responded by saying that the "I" stood for Incomplete, and there was no mistake. He told me that he "caught" my attempt to turn in a final lab report from my previous class for his last assignment and that he reported me to academic conduct for plagiarism. He went on to say that the "I" would be there until they reviewed my case and determined if I had plagiarized—which would lead to me failing his course and more than likely being expelled from the university.

My professor's response was shocking, but I realized I must have mistakenly uploaded "lab report 8" from my previous course instead of the "lab report 8" from my current one. It was a simple mistake caused by me accidentally saving lab reports under the same name on my computer. The lab reports were on two completely different topics, so it wouldn't make logical sense for me to turn in a report from a previous course in place of my actual assignment for this class. I trusted that once I explained the error, this misunderstanding would be over. He responded to my explanation, with a request that I send him the correct lab report immediately. Within ten minutes, I sent him the accurate lab report once I located it on my computer. My professor wrote back within minutes saying that he checked the last save date and time on the document, and it showed the report was saved only moments ago, so I must have just done the report. Therefore, he was moving forward with the allegations.

I was stunned. And now, I was also enraged. I was trying to give my professor the benefit of the doubt before. Now, I realized that he was attempting to jeopardize my standing with the university, and he believed that I plagiarized in such an obvious, thoughtless way. I thought my sociology professor was bad, but this professor's behavior was one of the most passive-aggressive actions I had experienced from anyone in my educational career. My professor was unaware that I was a very involved student on campus and had just been elected the vice president of the Emory University student government. I interfaced with Emory administration consistently, including the dean who oversaw academic conduct. I also knew that as a university policy, professors must notify students before reporting them for a conduct violation—which my professor failed to do.

I was shaking from anger. *How dare he attempt to destroy my academic standing without even giving me the decency of a conversation beforehand.* I immediately began to write him an email that outlined my various involvements on campus, indicating I had too much to lose to plagiarize in such an obvious way. I also reminded him that I passed this course previously with a different professor and only wanted to retake his course for a better grade, and by the time of the last assignment, I had already achieved that. I asked him: Why would I go through such lengths to submit a lab report that was not even on the same topic as the assignment? I wanted to show him how absurd his rationale was. At the end of the email, I demanded that he set up a meeting with the dean overseeing conduct. We all could discuss the matter in person. He responded with a short message saying he would set up the appointment.

A week went by, and I had not heard any update from him regarding the meeting. During the week, I spoke with a couple of deans on campus to outline what happened, and each of them told me that the professor had violated the policy by not telling me he was reporting me to academic conduct. And they were shocked with how he was handling the situation. They assured me any dean would correct the problem immediately. I wrote a follow-up email to my professor asking him if he had set up our meeting with the dean of academic conduct, but he did not reply. In my frustration, I wrote him another email telling him that since he could not do his job, I would; I had already contacted various deans about the situation and would schedule the meeting with the dean of academic conduct myself. I also informed him that everyone I spoke with was shocked that a professor would accuse a student of plagiarism and submit them to academic conduct without first informing them. Lastly, I told him that I was sure the dean of academic conduct would be interested to hear his rationale for breaking university policy.

Astonishingly, my last email got an immediate response from him. He wrote that he thought it over and decided he would drop the allegations against me and use the last lab report I turned in for his class before the final as the grade for my final exam. He said I should expect my final grade to be in the system within days.

Looking back, I honestly believe my professor had assumed I was just another Black student who he could easily disregard, a student who would not advocate for themself. I am glad I proved him wrong. I thought my issue with my sociology professor would have been unique, but now I knew I had to be more vigilant in protecting myself in the academic space at Emory. If my psychology professor taught me nothing else, he taught me that some of the professors in this elite higher education space were out for blood— that is, the blood of the students they believed did not belong there.

Today, as an administrator in higher education, I unfortunately see similar scenarios play out. Students of color often complain about being unfairly graded and treated poorly by White faculty. Over a decade later, not much has changed. I hope that by sharing stories like the ones I shared above, stories that are sadly not unique, I provide a microscope that magnifies what happens on college campuses all across our country.

———

EDUCATION HAS BEEN a source of personal liberation throughout human history. Nelson Mandela said, "Education is the most powerful weapon which you can use to change the world." I think this is especially true for higher education. One of the aspects I love most about college is how its intellectual environment has allowed for some of the greatest teachings in liberation and freedom movements in recent history. Brilliant minds from past and present have used college campuses and classes as a launching pad to inspire radical works that challenge oppressive systems and demand change within society. Many of the people who have personally inspired me have had some of their most meaningful ideas spread through universities. Or their work itself was something they created or imagined at a college or university.

As I continue to think about solutions that could move us out of this social and racial caste system that exists in education, I think higher education institutions play a crucial role in that effort. I had my fair share of experiences in my own college years that illustrate the potential powerful role of higher education in fostering radical change as well as the vast inequities that still exist within colleges and universities across the country.

During my time at Emory, the course Race and Ethnic Relations offered by the sociology department was pivotal for me. I never had a class that taught me an authentic representation of racial history in America. The class was my first introduction to the history behind many of my lived experiences. As I learned about the social constructions of race for political reasons, redlining discriminatory practices that created housing disparities for many Black Americans, the intentional criminalization of Black people throughout history, and so on, I felt a sense of liberation. I finally put theory and evidence behind many of my experiences and the legacy of my family members around me. It was as if up until this point, I had been in a battle without armor, but my Race and Ethnic Relations class began to provide me with the training and equipment that I needed to be more successful in war.

I loved it. *The New Jim Crow* by Michelle Alexander was a particularly transformational reading. Alexander's work resonated deeply within me because of my experiences with my father and the criminal justice system. We even had the opportunity to listen to her speak in our class, and she brought life to the words that we read and inspired our class like no other guest speaker. After that semester, my passion for justice was newly ignited, and there was no turning back.

As I contemplated racial disparities in America on the heels of my Race and Ethnic Relations course and thought about the hopelessness I saw in many people I knew growing up, I was troubled. I realized this was the reason I was so interested in psychology. These contemplations gave birth to my desire to find ways to wed my interests to a passion project. I started to share my interest with some of my friends in the student government, and our chief of staff introduced me to Christine Ristaino.

Christine was a professor of Italian culture and language and taught in the educational studies department. She often partnered with educational organizations in the broader Atlanta community that supported Black and Brown students. One school was the Ron Clark Academy, a nationally known private school predominantly serving low-income Black students. I was excited to meet her and share my ideas.

In our first meeting, I told her my vision for creating a curriculum for children that countered the learned helplessness that I saw growing up from those in my community. She was intrigued by my ideas and asked me more questions. After the two of us spoke, we felt inspired and genuinely connected. She agreed to take me on as a student mentee to help me realize my vision.

I worked on an independent research study with Professor Ristaino for three semesters. I researched the Reggio Emilia approach to early childhood development, learned helplessness, and self-efficacy development. From this, I developed a six-week curriculum entitled the *L.I.F.E. Curriculum* that focused on developing and cultivating Leadership, Individuality, Freedom, and Empowerment in students, specifically Black and Brown students. Professor Ristaino provided feedback and insights as I designed the curriculum. My independent study was a transformational experience; one that, unbeknownst to me at the time, would set me up for a career in education.

When I reflect back on these transformational experiences in my time at the university, it reaffirms my assertion that higher education institutions have immense power to drive change in America, and specifically in determining the framework for educating individuals in this country. If we move away from the traditions, cultural norms, and inequitable practices, we can begin to uncover the untapped potential we have on university campuses across the country.

———————

THOUGH UNIVERSITIES HAVE immense potential to right their wrongs, today most still operate with inherent inequities. One of the major shortcomings that has been highlighted in mainstream conversations recently is how highly selective universities admit their students and how this process constructs a student body that further isolates students of color and other marginalized identities. Though there has been more focus on how elite universities ensure more diversity in admissions, there are still a substantial number of policies and tactics that determine who gets into these schools and who is kept out. According to a 2020 Wall Street Journal report, "56 percent of the nation's top 250 institutions consider legacy in their admissions process." This means that students whose parents or other family members went to a university are more likely to get accepted to that university. Often these students come from White, higher socioeconomic backgrounds and get a further advantage merely by having a family member who was an alum. A Harvard Graduate School of Education study conducted in 2007 on thirty highly selective colleges found that "legacy applicants were three times more likely to be admitted as equally qualified non-legacy applicants." Even today, at Harvard University specifically, legacy applicants are six times more likely to be admitted than non-legacy or non-athlete applicants. Further, the percentage of legacy admits in the freshman classes of several top colleges across the country outweighs the percentage of Black freshman admitted altogether at those same colleges. If the recent and unfortunate affirmative action decision brings anything positive into society, my hope is that legacy admission continues to be questioned and challenged and rethought to be more equitable.

However, when you take into account athlete admissions, donation-based admissions, as well as legacy admissions and compare them to the number of students admitted by the now-banned race-conscious admissions, the latter pales in comparison at highly selective institutions. What's even worse, in my opinion, is that besides the factors I have mentioned, most highly selective universities admit students who come from expensive, elite private high schools at an extremely high rate. At some colleges, upward of 30 percent of their incoming class comes from these privileged high schools. The disproportionate nature of this number is more staggering when one realizes only 2 percent of all high school students in America attend these elite high schools. This practice continues to perpetuate a social hierarchy of the "ruling class." Individuals with money, status, and access continue to attain power in our society through education at elite institutions. This arrangement upholds the brutal and cutthroat "competitive" practices that White supremacy sustains itself on. If the student makeup at these elite higher education institutions consists predominantly of a particular type of student, a student that comes from environments grounded in White supremacy and elitism, then one can imagine what quality of peer environment that creates for students who do not come from such backgrounds.

———

I MYSELF EXPERIENCED discriminatory actions from my peers while at Emory. In light of my successful initiatives as SGA vice president and my reputation as a dynamic resident advisor (RA), many students suggested that I run for student government president. The last and only time Emory University had a Black student government president had been twelve years ago, in the year 2000, so I felt like it was an opportunity for long overdue representation.

I began to gear up for the campaign. I wanted to organize a campaign team that I felt represented all students on campus. I had students from Emory's Hillel—the Jewish student group—Black

Student Association, Muslim Student Association, Graduate Student Government Association, fraternities, sororities, and Emory's Indian Cultural Exchange (ICE), just to name a few, working on my campaign. I felt like I had all my bases covered.

I knew it would be a tough race because I was running against the current college council president, Parth. Unlike many of my other Indian American friends at Emory, Parth had a stronger affinity to White culture on campus. He was not a member of any of the Indian cultural groups. However, he was in a popular predominantly White fraternity known as the "leadership" fraternity and was well regarded by students and administration on campus. White fraternity and sorority life on Emory's campus was a significant part of the student experience. At the time, roughly 33 percent of undergraduate students participated in Greek life, and it was a big part of the social dynamics on campus and the most significant driver of the elite White atmosphere of the peer experience. The predominantly White fraternities had a reputation for being particularly racist toward Black students on campus. For instance, Black girls would generally not be allowed into parties thrown by White fraternities. Also, one fraternity, Kappa Alpha, had a portrait of the confederate leader General Robert E. Lee hanging up in their frat house at the time.

One night, during Emory's annual costume party called Dooley's Ball, a group of White guys tried to barricade their door and not let me in their frat house. I was dressed up as Tupac. Many younger members of the fraternity (ZBT) assumed I was not a student, and I was on campus to "cause trouble." It wasn't until an upper-class frat brother of theirs who was a friend of mine came to the door because of the commotion, realized what they were doing, and yelled at them, "That's Brian Fuller, you idiots!" that they backed away from the door and let me in.

I knew that Greek life had a significant influence on campus, but I also knew I did, too. I spent the next few weeks diligently campaigning. I leveraged my friendships with many people in the fraternities and sororities. I visited dorms at night to meet with students, went to events at the business school, graduate schools, and student organizations to speak about my platform. I was everywhere. I hung up banners across campus and placed campaign flyers in as many places as possible. I was feeling hopeful about my efforts, but I also felt the pressure from my opponent.

As the campaign was ending, the president of the SGA decided to let me send out the university-wide newsletter so I "could get practice" as he kindly put it. As an ally, he was strongly hoping I would win. As vice president, I was well within my right to send out the letter to all students in place of the president of SGA at any time. However, my opponent did not think so. He felt that this gave me a leg up because of name recognition. He and a couple of his supporters filed a complaint against me with the elections board in hopes of getting me disqualified. That's when I realized they were willing to go to any length to win.

Two days before voting, the *Emory Wheel*, Emory's student-led newspaper, hosted a presidential debate. During the debate, Parth kept taking my talking points from other campaign speeches and videos and using them as his own. Because he went first, he would say something from my platform before I would have an opportunity to say it. I was upset, but I kept my cool.

After the debate, the newspaper staff deliberated about which candidate to endorse for hours. Later that night, the *Emory Wheel* released an article online with the headline WHEEL ENDORSEMENT: BRIAN FULLER: INNOVATIVE AND ENTHUSIASTIC. Their backing was crucial. I now had the most visibility possible going into the election. There were only a couple of more days before voting, and I was riding high.

The following morning, I woke up excited to get a hard copy of the *Wheel* to read the article from late the night before. As I left my dorm room and walked across the quad, I noticed all of my campaign flyers were gone. Even the banner that I had hung in the middle of campus had been ripped and torn down. *What happened?! Who did this?!* I then started to receive text messages from friends to inform me that every sign of mine on campus was no longer up. A group of individuals must have torn them down late the previous night.

To make matters worse, my friends began to tell me that there was a firestorm in the comments online under my endorsement article. I quickly took out my laptop to log in and went to the article. There were negative comments below the article page, all from anonymous students. It seemed as if some group flooded the comment section with negativity. Not only were the remarks negative, but the majority of them were racist. I quickly skimmed through comments that said, "the only reason he got endorsed is because he's Black—he's not the best candidate." "Brian is not even smart enough to be SGA president." "They are only endorsing him because right now it looks good to support Black people, he doesn't deserve it." Some comments contained the racial slur "nigger."

Our campus was already particularly sensitive to race because of the recent murder of Trayvon Martin. The comments were cruel. I was in shock. Many of my friends started to go in the comments to defend me, but I told them to stop because the anonymous opinions of people did not matter. Eventually, the newspaper disabled the comment section.

Now, in the final hour of the campaign, everything was falling apart. I had no signs up on campus, there had been myriad negative comments under my endorsement, and I also had to go to an election board hearing because of the complaint Parth had filed. The complaint was a dirty tactic because it would automatically disqualify me from the race if I did not show up for the hearing. And the hearing prevented me from actively campaigning until the elections board determined the verdict. I was stuck.

After class, I went to my elections board hearing prepared to argue that I did not violate any policy. To my surprise, Parth did not show up, so the board dismissed the complaint. However, the damage was already done. The hearing had kept me from being able to campaign or replace my signs in the last hour. After the hearing, I walked through campus, saw Parth's campaign signs for president, and was reminded that all of mine were now gone. When I arrived back at my room, I felt defeated.

I felt defeated and I felt flattened. Back in my dorm room, I began to cry. I cried because of the cruelty of the comments. I cried because even though I had worked so hard, my effort now seemed to be all in vain. I cried because, at that moment, I realized I had given so much of myself to a student body that had reduced me to racial slurs and ignorant punchlines. I cried because I realized Emory was no different than the rest of the world, no matter how much I wanted it to be, and perhaps it was even more shrouded in Whiteness. I cried because I realized the hard truth—being a Black student on an elite college campus did not exclude me from American White supremacy; in fact, the White background heightened the scrutiny.

The next day, after voting was completed, the elections board announced that Parth had won the election. He beat me by a slight margin of one hundred votes. At least, the horror story of the election was finally over.

MONTHS LATER THERE was another event that was a reminder to me and many other university students of color that elite American universities did not consider us or our histories as worthy of full presence in these particular spaces.

"As American as...Compromise" was the title of the now infamous article published in *Emory Magazine* that sparked a national uproar. The article was written by Emory University's president, James Wagner. Like many within the Emory community, I was disappointed when I read his words that used the three-fifths compromise, the 1787 constitutional agreement that determined that slaves would count as three-fifths of a person, as a supposedly shining example of compromise. Here was yet another racially charged blunder at an elite, American university.

What was more deeply troubling to me was that President Wagner released this essay partly in response to one of many "compromises" on the horizon at Emory. The university had announced plans to make academic cuts that disproportionately affected students and faculty of color during the previous year. One of the divisions slated for removal was the Division of Educational Studies, the department with the highest percentage of Black students within the university, at roughly 40 percent.

In his article, President Wagner highlighted the three-fifths compromise as a high point in our nation's history, a moment that brought together competing ideals for the common good. He posited that Emory needed to engage in the same types of "compromise" to reach the "highest aspirations" of the university.

Understandably the students, and the public at large, were outraged. How could Wagner see slaveholding as a legitimate "ideal" to be upheld? Some students and faculty called for Wagner's resignation. I shared some of the sentiments of that collective, but, candidly, I was conflicted.

By now, as a senior in my final semester, I was known as a student leader by students and the administration. Consequently, I had come to know President Wagner on a personal level, through my various leadership roles on campus. Unlike my previous experience with White male educators in my high school, I found Wagner to be thoughtful, warm, welcoming, and insightful. So, I was torn when I read the article and heard the outcry from classmates and university faculty. *How could he not know that his words were a gross mistake? How could the editors and team around him not recognize the impact his words would have on the Black community? How could he not be sensitive to race in this country? Should the community allow him the opportunity to correct his wrongs?* My thoughts were swirling.

A couple of days after the article was published, President Wagner released an apology and update to the piece. He apologized for his "clumsiness and insensitivity." He clarified his stance on slavery, calling it "heinous, repulsive, inhuman, and repugnant." He also asked a group of student leaders of color to meet with him so he could "listen and learn." I was one of those students.

In the meeting, I witnessed some of my classmates, mostly friends, share stories of feeling unwanted at the university and shed tears, indicating that they felt the need to constantly fight to prove their "right" to be there. I was angry as I listened to my classmates

speak, share, and cry as President Wagner appeared to listen empa-
thetically. *How could they give him the satisfaction to think that his
words were important enough to impact them? How could they say they
felt like they did not belong on campus?* My mind and emotions traveled back to high school. There was no way in hell I was going to
let this White man get satisfaction in seeing me sweat. And I was
not about to shed any tears in front of him. Like my classmates in
the meeting, I had experienced many adverse and racist events at
Emory, but unlike them, none of those experiences had made me
feel undeserving or as if I did not belong on campus. Looking back
now, I commend my classmates for their vulnerability at that moment and for revealing their experiences. Now I can appreciate
what they did.

That said, I truthfully was underwhelmed by the performative
nature of this entire ordeal. When I finally decided to speak, I shared
that growing up in Sumter, South Carolina, I experienced "overt racism" frequently. At Emory, I continued, I had "not experienced" this
level of direct prejudice (although I had at times). I stated it clearly
and calmly: I knew I belonged. I was unwilling to reveal the extent
of racism I had experienced on campus if it meant I had to perform
a version of Black pain for this White authority figure. I deserved
to be at Emory, and I never doubted that regardless of the circumstances around me. I left the meeting with one of my best friends
at Emory, a Nigerian American woman, and I explained my annoyance with what we had just experienced. She felt the same.

As I reflect now, I find it ironic that "As American as…Compro-
mise" was the title that President Wagner chose for his column.
Compromise is indeed at the foundation of America—merging
competing ideals is what our country was built on. That is true.
But I think the example that Wagner chose to support his argu-
ments speaks volumes. Likening Black people to three-fifths of a
person, in other words assuming falsely that Black people are sub-
human, is *the moral compromise* found at the foundation of our
country. And, as I was experiencing, by extension the foundation
of the systems put in place to educate us.

Although Wagner expressed what I believe was his sincere regret for the "insensitivity" of the article, I think that his careless mistake was actually a Freudian slip. It revealed his true mindset he would not have otherwise stated. The article was a representation of the unconscious bias of not only President Wagner but of those who lead, uphold, and trust in our traditional systems of education, a bias which holds Black and marginalized people to be less than fully human.

The historical evidence shows America's K–12 educational experience perpetuates a racial and social hierarchy, and that this hierarchy further establishes itself in institutions of higher education. One need not look further than Nikole Hannah-Jones's *1619 Project* for a detailed analysis. Therefore, it's not surprising that 1787's three-fifths compromise was the first that came to Wagner's mind when thinking about the necessary compromise that needed to take place to advance Emory University's priorities. The words written in 1787 by the leaders of this country were inscribed in a culture that had already established Black people as inferior, a culture that left their voices and perspectives unacknowledged.

Likewise, when President Wagner and his team at *Emory Magazine* wrote the words of that article, they were doing so in a culture of elite higher educational institutions that had already established Black (and Brown) inferiority. Thus, the article "As American As… Compromise" was a predictable product of the American higher education ecosystem just as the three-fifths compromise of 1787 was a predictable product of the early American ecosystem.

———

DESPITE THE EVER-PRESENT challenges on college campuses for Black and marginalized students, I know college can be a place that provides opportunity, inspires new thinking, and transforms a student's life. I know this because such pivotal change came unexpectedly to me through a tremendously empowering conversation I will never forget.

As an Emory tradition, Jimmy Carter held an annual dinner with student leaders and faculty on campus, before delivering an address to the freshman class. As the student government vice president, I was to be seated at the same table as President Carter with two other student leaders. My nerves heightened a bit when I came into the ballroom and realized I did not get the memo that one must wear a dark suit when meeting the POTUS. Not only was I one of two Black guys in the room, but I was also sporting a light tan suit with a pink undershirt and colorful tie, the only suit I owned at the time. Needless to say, I stood out. After a few snide comments from other students about my outfit, it was time to sit down for dinner.

The table was silent for a moment. I did not know if I was going to speak. Then my classmates started to ask questions. It seemed like they were trying to prove how smart they were by asking about foreign policy, the US economy, and other political topics. I felt like we were in an academic class rather than having dinner with the former leader of the free world.

I listened, laughed at jokes, and nodded along, but I was still in my head. However, in my silent observations, I got the sense that President Carter was also annoyed with the bravado of my two classmates. He seemed as if he talked about these topics all the time, and it was boring him. Nonetheless, he was cordial and answered graciously but did not seem like he enjoyed the discussion. And, candidly, I didn't either. I wanted to know about Jimmy Carter as a person. *What was his mentality growing up? Did he always know that he wanted to be president? How does he feel about his impact now after the presidency?*

Trusting my intuition, I decided to interject. "President Carter, as a child, did you dream of being president one day? Was that something you always wanted?" He looked at me with intrigue and said no, that was not what he dreamed of as a child. He then shared about how he grew up in rural Georgia as a sharecropper during the Jim Crow era and always felt a sense of injustice in the world because he considered himself the same as the Black people who lived around him. I wondered if he mentioned race because I was there. I connected with his story and shared with him that my grandparents grew up as sharecroppers in rural South Carolina. My comments lit him up, and he talked more about how he wanted to be involved in his younger years because of the injustices in the world and knew he wanted to make a difference in his community. Then he went on to say that he never considered being president until his team presented the idea to him while he was governor of Georgia.

The dinner was nearing an end, and as he was leaving, he looked at me and thanked me for a great conversation. He then thanked all three of us at the table. We thanked him for his time and said it was such a pleasure to meet him. I was thrilled! This dinner turned out not to be a disaster after all.

MY TIME AT Emory was ending, and most of my family had come to town for my graduation. Even my father was there. Because President Obama's administration decided to retroactively apply the Fair Sentencing Act, a piece of 2010 legislation that reduced the 100:1 disparity between crack cocaine and powder cocaine sentencing to 18:1, my father's sentence had been dramatically reduced. By the spring of 2012, he had served his time. My college graduation was the first instance that my entire family, including my father, would be together to celebrate. And, as my family would soon see, I had established myself as a crucial member of my community.

My family witnessed the many honors and awards for hard work and service that I received during graduation weekend. I was bursting with joy. My grandparents, parents, aunts, uncles, and cousins heard deans, professors, fellow students, and members of the board of trustees speak highly about me. Many made a point to compliment me and my family. This experience touched my heart in ways I can't fully express. I have always had a desire to honor my family. I understand them intimately—their pains, their struggles, their insecurities, and how society has picked them apart. I understand their hopes, their dreams, and I have always wanted to make them proud and honor them with my life. And that weekend, I believed I did just that. People at Emory respected my family because these same people there had come to respect me. Their demonstration of respect meant everything. No one knew about my father's incarceration—they simply congratulated him on raising a great son. No one knew my mother's struggles, my grandparents' perseverance, my uncles' and aunts' doubts. Rather, they simply respected them because of my accomplishments. The respect my family received meant more to me than any of the awards given.

As a final honor, Emory's administration selected me to lead the graduation procession by carrying the Emory University gonfalon, or heraldic flag, during the ceremony. As part of the duty, I was given the opportunity to sit on the main stage. While up there, I experienced a sense of pride. *I know I belong here.* As I think back to that bright, sunny, cool morning in May, I undoubtedly understood I deserved the honor. My sense of self-worth was a common thread while at Emory—regardless of the beliefs or actions of those around me.

Candidly, though, I often think about those who felt differently and the underlying meaning of the words "the only reason he got endorsed is because he's Black." Those words most poignantly represent my hardest challenge at Emory and the towering challenge for Black and other marginalized people in these spaces. The implication behind the phrase holds a sting as powerful as the sting of my White classmate who told me during my freshman year that I was "just another case of affirmative action." I believe the challenges that I and many other marginalized students faced at Emory stemmed from the notion that we somehow were "lucky to be there" and inevitably we did not deserve the opportunity. We were there out of performative necessity but not because we were wanted and surely not because we truly earned it. My two professors reiterated this notion in their attempt to undermine my academic success. Even Emory's president, James Wagner, reiterated this idea in his controversial essay and by supporting the decision of the programmatic cuts. Many students reiterated this sentiment with their discriminatory actions and words against their Black classmates, including myself.

I must acknowledge that the culture of elite higher education in America breathes life into and feeds this flawed idea, a culture that does not genuinely value the Black person and their contributions, a culture intentionally established in the American K–12 education system that precedes it.

Therefore, when I, a Black man, entered Emory, declared my right to be there, and had the audacity to lead, it rattled those who subscribed to the idea that Black people were there merely as an act of charity. It rattled them enough for them to attempt to remind me of my supposed "inferiority."

We can see this story play out outside of Emory many times on the national stage. For example, we see this in the controversy with the prominent Black American journalist Nikole Hannah-Jones in 2021, when she was denied tenure at her alma mater, the University of North Carolina. We see it in the 2019 college admissions scandal in California, where celebrities and wealthy parents bought and bribed their way into the higher education system. We see it in the numerous cases that led to the overturning of affirmative action policies, such as the *Students for Fair Admissions* lawsuit decided by the Supreme Court in 2023. We see it in higher education's inability to effectively integrate and support Black students and faculty with resources outside of performative gestures. The lack of acknowledgment of the value of the Black perspective and Black impact is pervasive throughout elite higher education spaces. But again, regardless of how others feel, *I know that all students, especially those Black and marginalized, deserve to be there.* W. E. B. Du Bois, when asked in 1890 if he was honored to be the first Black person to earn a PhD from Harvard University, said, "The honor, I assure you, was Harvard's."

I agree with his statement. His words continue to resonate around me today. Like Du Bois, I would say the following to any

Black or marginalized person who ever doubted their right to be in an elite higher education institution: even when the institution does not acknowledge how privileged they are to have you, I assure you—the honor is always theirs.

CHAPTER 7

A Dreamless Land

It is only for the sake of those without hope that hope is given to us.

—WALTER BENJAMIN, 1924

JULY 20, 2014

I felt like I was responsible for bringing these eight Black teenagers to the slaughter. My heart sank as I witnessed my worst fear play out in front of my eyes. I saw the devastation on their faces, and I knew this emotional experience would confirm the worst ideas they had about themselves, school, and the world. *What had I done?*

We were in the famous Harvard Square, with its stately buildings and aloof undergraduates strolling purposefully. By "we" I mean myself, the founder of The DREAM Program, Inc., and eight Black teens from Philadelphia. We were on an exciting Northeastern college tour road trip through New Jersey, New York, Massachusetts, and Vermont. Now I was feeling intense regret about bringing them here to Harvard. Ironically, I was the one who pushed for the storied university to be on the itinerary when we planned the trip. I wanted the teens, who mostly had never left their neighborhoods in Philadelphia, to experience the "best university" in the world. I wanted them to know that they could go there, too.

The teens—three girls and five boys from North and West Philadelphia—were a part of our mentor-in-training program at the educational nonprofit DREAM, and all had significant challenges with school. Many of them had been expelled from traditional public schools in Philly and were now in alternative educational situations. The eldest teen, a boy named Lewis, just graduated from high school and was the first person in his family to accomplish that feat but already had significant experience with the criminal justice system. In fact, in order for him to take the trip out of state, Lewis's parole officer had to give their approval.

I spent time before and during the van ride lecturing the teens about how to "properly present themselves" to people as we toured college campuses. I told them to act "happy and be polite," to "smile and come across as friendly," and to "not scare people away." Remnants of the respectability politics instilled in me as a Black child growing up in the South still had a deep hold on me. I believed that teaching these teens to behave more "appropriately" and carry themselves "well" would mitigate any negative interactions we had with other people—especially White adults. I wanted to protect them. But I soon learned that I couldn't.

I shattered when I witnessed the teens being ignored, scoffed at, and received with snobbery and disgust as they asked people in Harvard Square for directions. Just thirty minutes earlier, we had released the teens, giving them some freedom to explore the square on their own. The program's founder and I left to set up the logistics for the official campus tour, which was scheduled for after lunch. We set a time for everyone to reunite at the well-known Bartley's Burgers. I once again reminded them about "how to interact with people" while we were not around.

As the time was nearing for us to come back together, the teens got lost and began to ask individuals walking in Harvard Square for the restaurant's location. I happened to be walking up about fifty feet behind the teens as they were asking for help and directions. I witnessed the teens smile and approach people with calm, kind demeanors just as I instructed them. And I watched as what I assumed were Harvard students, professors, and staff treat the teens horribly. I watched White adults become fearful, physically move out of the way like they were avoiding a plague, blatantly ignore them, or appear visibly disgusted. One White person after another dismissed the teens while they kept desperately and sincerely asking for directions. I saw the teens' faces fill with defeat with each person's negative response.

As I watched, I was devastated and shocked. And I was angry. I wanted to expose those people for how they were interacting with these teenagers, these kids. *How dare they be so inhumane, so callous?* I also was angry with myself because I had told the teens that their behavior impacted how the world interacted with them. I had told them they had to change aspects of their personalities to be treated with decency. And what I had told them was now proven to be untrue. In my frustration with the situation, I yelled out one of the teens' names to get her attention. For my own mental sanity, I needed them to immediately stop asking for help. The teens assumed I was angry with them, but I wasn't. I was only frustrated with the situation, with myself, and my emotions got the best of me. Frankly, I was devastated. I gathered the teens together and we went to lunch.

After lunch, I apologized to the eight youngsters in a conversation in the park. I told them I was sorry for misguiding them. I also said to them that sometimes people would dislike them just because of who they are, and people who subscribe to that mentality are ignorant. I went on to say that they should never think less of themselves because of what others think of them. I reinforced that they were amazing and had a right to be anywhere. The teens responded that they were "okay" and knew the "Harvard people would be bougie and stuck-up." Discriminatory actions from adults were normalized in their experience. The teens like myself, and other Black kids in this country, were all too familiar with prejudice, racism, and mistreatment. They probably had experienced it even more than I had. And similar to me throughout my life, they just wanted to move on from this adverse experience and continue with their day.

I revisit that moment in Harvard Square often. It was my first conscious realization that I, as a product of my American education, had beliefs and internalized oppression that could harm other Black kids like me. My difficult school experiences had left an impression on me, and I thought my only goal was to help others not have those same experiences. But was I mistaken?

I started to contemplate the ways that I learned to dishonor myself as a means for my safety and success in the system. I had spent the past year with the teens and the other children at DREAM, challenging some of their authentic ways of being, requesting that they change even unharmful expressions all under the guise of wanting to protect them. I hoped to make their experience less damaging. However, my ways could have inevitably articulated to them that they, in some ways, did not belong in certain spaces because of who they were. That their being themselves was not enough. Society had already told them the same message all of their lives, a message I so desperately had fought against in school. Had my actions with the teens unintentionally stifled their aspirations? Until this point, I thought I was somehow immune to the miseducation of Black people in schools because I had reached a high level of academic achievement. And if others adopted my mindset, they could reach that level, too. However, I realized that the gross miseducation that happened to us Black people was deeply ingrained in me. And, candidly, my realization at this moment only scratched the surface of the early miseducation I had internalized.

ANY EDUCATOR WILL tell you that one of the most significant challenges in our education system is trying to address the multitude of American societal ills in our schools. Issues like widespread poverty, poor housing conditions, under-resourced neighborhoods, lack of mental health resources, and inaccessible healthcare are realities that millions of American children experience outside of our schools but have a direct impact on what manifests in our public schools. Poverty has become one of the most prevalent indicators of academic achievement in our schools today. Children living in poverty are more likely to attend under-resourced schools and are more likely to have poor academic performance. And to no one's surprise, Black, Latino, and Asian children are much more likely to experience poverty than their White counterparts in America.

As I stated in the beginning of this book, I strongly believe that to begin to understand how our schools can better serve all students, we must fully understand their lived experiences. This also means understanding what it means to exist in poverty daily and what that does to one's aspirations, motivations, and willingness to learn. Poverty is an ever-present societal ill and has racial and cultural implications that continue to perpetuate a vicious cycle in our education system. For me it was not until I began my work in Philadelphia, the location of the highest poverty rate of our nation's most populous cities, that I started to understand the devastation poverty can have on a community and how that is so inextricably linked to the public education that those in that community are experiencing.

SEPTEMBER 2013

After I graduated from Emory, I landed what I felt was a dream job at an organization, coincidentally called DREAM. I was hired as the founding program director for the Philadelphia region of The DREAM Program, Inc. DREAM was founded in 1999, and later incorporated in 2001, by two Dartmouth College graduates who had been mentoring youth at a local Section Eight housing unit within the community. DREAM developed into an organization that pairs undergraduate college students with children living in public housing for "village mentoring, group adventures, academic support, and more." I was elated when I accepted the role. I was the only hire for the Philadelphia region of the organization at the time, so I would essentially be starting from scratch. We had secured a major grant from the well-known Philadelphia Housing Authority (PHA) and a smaller public housing management company, Ingerman Group. We would be supporting children living in three communities across North and West Philadelphia. However, I had not yet established a presence in any housing community, nor had I made the necessary local partnerships with the universities. And I was completely new to Philadelphia. I had my work cut out for me.

Also, I was unaware of the backdrop of chaos happening with the school system at the time. Earlier that year, in June, the School District of Philadelphia had cut over three thousand employees and closed twenty-four schools because of a lack of financial resources. The district, which was roughly 69 percent Black and Latino at the time, had even considered not opening schools if they did not receive emergency funding from the state. The district superintendent, William Hite, argued that the schools needed the funding so staff could ensure schools could run safely for the students. As I arrived in the city, the hysteria surrounding the school system's challenges played out in the children's day-to-day lives.

It is hard for me to articulate how jarring the first few weeks in Philadelphia were. I had just come from living in a bubble at Emory University for four years, where the prestigious environment shielded me from many of the harsh realities of the world, especially the realities of poverty that many Black and Brown Americans experience. My time at Emory distanced me from my foundation in Sumter in many ways. However, being in Philadelphia was a loud wake-up call back to that reality.

As a function of the PHA grant that we received, DREAM was responsible for the youth programming in two of the largest high-rise public housing units in Philadelphia. The biggest was Westpark Apartments in West Philadelphia, with 363 units spanning three high-rise towers. The second largest was Fairhill Apartments in North Philadelphia, with 264 units across two high-rise towers and low-rise units behind the towers. I had never seen or experienced public housing towers before. Fairhill Apartments were on the south edge of the Fairhill neighborhood, which at the time was the poorest neighborhood in Philadelphia and had some of the highest crime rates in the city. And both the West and North Philly neighborhoods were almost fully Black and Latino.

As I began to explore and get to know the communities I would be working in, I was floored by what I saw and experienced. As I was taking in my new environment, it seemed as if being Black in Philly was synonymous with pain and anguish. I witnessed addiction, violence, dilapidated apartments, poverty, and many other societal ills all in one place. In many ways, the pains, plights, and disenfranchisement that W. E. B. Du Bois described in his 1899 sociological study, *The Philadelphia Negro*, had remained the same for Black Philadelphians living under late capitalism. The intersecting problems of miseducation, "poverty, crime, and the dislike of the stranger," as Du Bois put it, appeared just as prevalent to me in North and West Philadelphia as they did to him in Philadelphia's all-Black Seventh Ward over a century ago. It was a way of life that seemed to be on a never-ending loop.

During my first few weeks on the job, the White senior leaders at the DREAM headquarters in Burlington, Vermont, encouraged me to go door-to-door daily in the public housing units. This tactic would allow me to introduce myself and the DREAM Program, and encourage folks to sign up their children for a new mentoring program in their community. I was told the door-to-door method had worked in other cities in Vermont and the Boston area, but I was unsure about this approach in Philly. I instinctively felt that Black people, or at least the ones I knew, did not like unannounced visits to their homes. Such a visit could be seen as disrespectful and met with defensiveness. Maybe the White and immigrant families living in public housing in Vermont were fine with random people knocking on their doors, but I wasn't convinced the Black and Latino people in Philly would be. And I didn't want to put myself in that line of fire. I was also keenly aware of what could happen if my identity was mistaken. I was an unknown young Black man walking around in these neighborhoods which many could see as threatening in ways that, candidly, the White DREAM leaders did not have to worry about. They stood out like a sore thumb in the community. Nevertheless, DREAM leadership pushed for me to "get out of my comfort zone" and go door-to-door. So, I did.

Pitching DREAM door-to-door was easiest in the Cecil B. Moore community. Cecil B. Moore was the smallest of the three sites made up of a small cluster of low-rise townhomes managed by the Ingerman Group. Some folks were hesitant, but generally, the people in the small community received me well. However, the response was just as I imagined it in the PHA-managed larger properties.

When I knocked on doors, with a smile and happy disposition, people often met me with hesitation, annoyance, or downright anger. One theme that kept coming up as I talked with various families living in the housing developments was their quick, almost knee-jerk acknowledgment that they knew I was not from Philly or their neighborhood. "Where are you from? I know you're not from around here," was a common phrase I would hear. Members of the communities would tell me I was too joyful or smiled too much to be from their community, making them wary of me. Their words brought me back to the feelings of ostracization that I felt in elementary school when the other Black kids treated me like an outsider. However, now I was a young adult, and I *actually was* the outsider. I was not from their community. I found it interesting that they would comment on my demeanor and say that I was "too happy" or "smiled too much" to be from the Philadelphia area or at least from their neighborhoods. I did not know it then, but this would be a reoccurring reaction that many of the kids who participated in DREAM would share with me as well. It was sad that joy was the emotion these kids and those in the community felt they could not show. I learned that their life experience was filled with so much adversity there was not much room for joy or happiness, only survival.

I learned a lot about these three communities going door-to-door. I saw the decrepit conditions of the Philadelphia Housing Authority's buildings. I saw the pain, anger, and sadness in the eyes of Black and Brown people that I encountered, and one clear thing was they did not trust me. I was a stranger coming into their community selling a dream for their kids like so many others before me who had tried and disappeared. When I reported back to Vermont about some of the challenges I was experiencing while "knocking on doors," the White senior leaders told me I needed to "stick it out." They said I should keep going even when I mentioned our approach felt unsafe. I was starting to feel that they did not understand the context. Or maybe even did not care to understand.

One White male senior leader, in particular, would come down to Philly from Burlington to support me for a day each week or every other week. I was excited about this because I wanted him to experience my perspective, and frankly, I needed the help. I could not wait to see how he handled the vaunted "door-to-door" approach in these high-rise Philadelphia towers. I was eager to learn from him.

One Friday, I suggested that we go to Westpark Apartments since it was our largest housing development, and candidly it was safer than Fairhill in North Philly. The two of us started early in the morning, going door-to-door. Most of the time, when we knocked on doors, no one answered. However, we finally got an answer from a young Black woman, who was not too thrilled by the sight of two men randomly knocking on her door at 11:00 A.M. She opened the door while on her cell phone, with visible irritation. At this point, I was accustomed to responses like this, but it was new for my colleague from DREAM. I turned to him, waiting for him to do our "pitch" and "win this parent over." He started to speak, but the woman was already in battle mode, cursing and combating anything he had to say. His face now was beet red, and he was visibly trembling. I guess this White man was not accustomed to not being welcomed with open arms at someone's door. I felt bad for him and wanted to intervene, but I just stood next to him as he tried to handle the situation. He was using his nicest "White voice" to explain that we were not selling anything but rather just talking about a program for the youth in the community. Finally, she let him get a word out, and she calmed a bit when she realized we had come in peace. She quickly just took our flyer for DREAM, thanked us, and shut the door. My colleague from DREAM, still shaken from the entire ordeal, decided to take a break for the rest of the day. His reaction was comical because this was the same person who expected me to do this for hours each day. If we were going to build a legitimate program in these communities, we needed a better approach.

THE PEW CHARITABLE TRUST states that more than 25 percent of Philadelphians live below the poverty line, a rate that is more than double the national average. And, more staggeringly, over 37 percent of Philadelphia's children are living in poverty. These children living in poverty are more likely to attend a district-led public school in the city and, according to the same study, over 75 percent of children who are living in poverty attend schools that received the lowest achievement rating by state standards. Though the numbers are inflated in Philadelphia, the trend is similar across the United States. Children living in poverty are more likely to attend public schools, and those public schools they attend are more likely to be underperforming by all measures.

I believe that many of the factors contributing to schools being deemed "underperforming" are steeped in White supremacy and a result of an inherently flawed education system. However, nonetheless, these are the schools that millions of children in America are attending. It is in the halls of these schools where millions of children are receiving an inadequate education that is not preparing or empowering them to be thriving American citizens. Further, attending these schools and living in these environments, I believe, considerably limits these children's aspirations, the possibilities that they can imagine for themselves, caging them in a vicious cycle of living out the same circumstances they see day in and day out. As children get older it becomes more apparent what an inadequate education and a lack of exposure to different experiences does to their psychology and outlook.

"YO! STOP CALLIN' my phone! I'm in an interview!" Malcolm yelled out to a teenage girl on the other end of his phone as we were sitting in the Westpark community center. He then hung up his cell phone, turned to me, and said, "Sorry about that, yo. This girl keeps calling me." He then nervously laughed.

The founder of DREAM and I were interviewing teens for our Philadelphia mentor-in-training program. We decided that we needed a new approach, and we discussed an idea to create a program where we would pay teens a small stipend to participate in DREAM to get the community and the kids rallied behind us. The teens knew their neighborhoods better than we did, and the younger kids looked up to them so it would incentivize participation. We would also engage in separate programming for the teens, and they would support our college-student mentors in weekly programming with our younger mentees.

Once I got the green light to move forward with this ground-up approach, I went to the resident council presidents of both Westpark and Fairhill. Both presidents were older Black women, old enough to be my grandmother, who had lived in their respective communities for most of their lives. They knew the neighborhood community inside and out and knew everything about everyone who lived there. I went to them and detailed our plan to hire teens in the neighborhood to support our programming efforts. I told them that I wanted "the most popular" teens in the neighborhood because they would help incentivize the kids to participate. In my conversations, each president laughed at me because they informed me the popular teens in the community were "the worst ones." I still pushed for those teens because I needed buy-in from the kids and other community members for DREAM to thrive. The college-student mentors would not have any mentees otherwise. The presidents obliged and gave the families of the teens our flyers to come to interviews for a new job opportunity for them in the neighborhood. We set up interviews in the evenings in the community centers of both Westpark and Fairhill, and the teens arrived.

Malcolm was a popular sixteen-year-old boy in Westpark and had an aggressive yet kind disposition. Like all the teens we spoke with, this was his first interview experience, so job interview etiquette was new to him. After his loud outburst during his phone conversation, I told him he needed to silence his phone and not answer it for the rest of the interview. We asked him a series of questions to get to know him better and understand his aspirations. One question we asked was, "What do you want to be when you grow up?"—a simple question that I hoped would shed light on the teens' aspirations and what they believed was possible.

Malcolm paused for a bit to think about it and said, "Umm, maybe a garbage man?"

This answer caught me off guard because I had never heard any kid say they hoped to be a sanitation worker before, but I thought, *Well, it is a stable job with a good pension, and they do get paid well.* So, I accepted his answer without question. He went on to mention other professions, too, like being a military officer, etc. After the interview ended, we asked Malcolm to join DREAM.

Over the next few days, the interviews continued. I met with several teens, including a set of sisters who both had dynamic energy that I thought would be perfect for the program. But as we continued the interviews, one pattern that emerged was the repeated answer I got from young boys to the same question we asked Malcolm, "What do you want to be when you grow up?" In both Westpark and Fairhill, most of the boys answered that question in the same way. They all would repeat, "I want to be a garbage man." The pattern was uncanny. I was trying to wrap my head around why all of these young men said the same thing. *Do they really all want to be garbage men?*

My curiosity got the best of me, and I finally asked one boy from Fairhill Apartments why he gave that specific answer and why I kept hearing the same response from other boys. He looked at me and said, "Well, the only two things I see around here are dealers and garbage men. The only dudes I know with a legit job are garbage men. And those dudes are the man, too. I'm not going to tell you that I want to be a dealer when I grow up, so I say I want to be a garbage man." He went on to tell me that's probably the reason other boys said the same thing.

His statements were eye-opening. I thought about myself in that moment and all of the aspirations that I had as a child and the dreams I currently had as an adult. They weren't limited, or at least I did not think they were. And the idea of my possibilities expanded as I continued to get older and have different and various experiences. I also thought about many Black men that I knew, including my father and a lot of the boys I grew up around who ended up in the criminal justice system. I thought about what their aspirations might have been growing up and how the world changed those aspirations over time. *What caused the change? Or did they never have aspirations from the start? What happened in their lives that narrowed their possibilities for themselves?* At that moment, I felt like I was in the right place. I knew I needed to be here with these kids. It was not because of what I could give to them but rather because of what they could give to me, what we could give to each other.

We wrapped up interviews and ended up with eight Black teens signed on for our mentor-in-training program. There were four boys, including two brothers from Fairhill—Lewis and Lamar. We hired Malcolm and another boy named Musa from Westpark. Also, there were four girls, including two sets of sisters, Amira and Amani from Fairhill and Tahiry and Majani from Westpark. More teens joined as the program grew. We were finally getting our program off the ground. The teens helped us get the word out in their respective communities. I spoke to the local universities near the housing communities we were established in—Temple University in North Philadelphia and the University of Pennsylvania in West Philadelphia. We started recruiting student mentors. The program was finally coming together, and it was time for us to get to work.

––––––––––

PROTECTING MYSELF, THE DREAM youth participants, the college-student mentors, and any other person affiliated with DREAM was a constant, top-of-mind priority as my time continued in Philadelphia. Violence was commonplace in the neighborhoods and the schools the DREAM children attended. I often would see young kids, elementary aged, from DREAM come to our programming with scratches or deep cuts on their faces and even the occasional bruises. Each time, without fail, the kids would tell their mentor or me that they had a fight at school or while walking home from school. Sometimes I would see these fights break out in the neighborhoods and, if I knew the kids, I would break them up.

Similarly, the teens I worked with would often reference their fights or the ones they were planning to have. It was like a badge of honor for them. Amira and Amani would mention they carried "blades in their buns," meaning they had a razor blade in their braided hairstyles just in case they needed to use it for protection. Lewis would carry around brass knuckles, and, truthfully, all the teenagers had access to guns. I would make them promise me that they would walk away from a fight if they could. I cared deeply about them and did not want to see them harmed in any way, at any time.

I felt the weighty responsibility for protecting these children because regardless of how society saw them—often as "scary" young adults—I knew they were just kids. And in my attempts to protect them and criticize their behaviors, I was hoping the world would see them as kids, too. But regardless, it was important to me that they knew I saw their innocence because I believe there was little to no opportunity in their daily experiences where they were granted that grace. Looking back, I hope that was liberating for them. Nevertheless, control and safety remained on my mind because I felt if anything slipped past me, it could endanger everyone. I was a young supervisor, and I needed to make sure everything was in order.

THE SUMMER HAD arrived, and we had endured our first school year of DREAM. The Philadelphia Housing Authority was impressed enough with our work that they extended our grant to provide a full summer camp at both Westpark and Fairhill. For the summer camp, I hired college-student mentors as interns, and we ran five-day-a-week summer programming for kids in both housing developments. As a part of the summer camp, we would often take kids on trips around the city. We would take them to museums, parks, and other Philadelphia attractions. Because I was becoming well known in the communities, I regularly engaged with parents, families, and community members while overseeing programming. My relationships with them led to the occasional participation of community members in our activities, including our field trips.

One particular man, Mecca, was the uncle of two of the members in DREAM and was popular in the Fairhill community. Interestingly, he also did some youth programming in Fairhill and aspired to expand. He would sometimes put on events and giveaways for the kids in the neighborhood. I was introduced to him when he organized a remembrance ceremony for his younger brother, who had been shot and killed. Mecca and I had built a cordial relationship as he would often check in with his niece and nephew during programming. More interestingly, Mecca was rumored to be a well-known "street pharmacist" in the community. I had never seen any of his "activities," but the teens told me about his dealings. However, I decided not to judge this choice too harshly because I knew from my own life experience that the circumstances people turn to in order to provide for themselves and their families are often nuanced. That said, it became clear to me there were times when Mecca felt the need to express his frustrations with DREAM's presence in the community, frustrations I suspected stemmed from his own desire to do similar work that had a visible and tangible impact. Already, I had to ask him not to join future DREAM programming because of how he chose to overstep and verbally discipline children harshly and unnecessarily on a field trip.

One day, while I was at Westpark Apartments, one of the interns from Fairhill called to tell me that Mecca was outside participating in our summer camp programming. The intern said she asked him to leave as I had instructed, but he would not. All the interns were scared to say anything else to him. I told them not to say anything more, and that I was on my way. During my train ride over to Fairhill, I was irritated. I thought Mecca and I had an understanding, and I knew that if he behaved harshly toward another kid that it could escalate and involve their families, which could put everyone's safety at risk.

When I arrived at Fairhill, I came up to the park where the interns were engaging in programming activities with the kids, and I saw Mecca sitting on a nearby bench watching the programming as if he were overseeing it. I went up to him, and he looked up at me, smiled, and said, "What's up, B? I'm surprised you're over here today. I thought you would have been at your other site in West Philly." I told him that I decided to come check in at Fairhill quickly, and I asked him if we could step aside from the kids to talk for a minute.

Once we got far away from the kids, I looked at him and said, "I thought we agreed that you would not be out here anymore, Mecca. What's up?"

Puzzled, he said, "You said that, but I never agreed. So, I just decided that I will keep participating how I normally was."

I gave him a confused look. I was growing more irritated because I felt maybe he was intentionally trying to be difficult. I responded, "Well, you did agree yesterday, and you can't keep participating, Mecca. I already told you that."

He looked at me with a smile and said, "Yes, I can. And I will." *What's happening? Am I being tricked? Does he think this is some type of joke?* I was trying to maintain a calm appearance.

We looked at each other intensely, almost without blinking. He went on to say, "This is my neighborhood, Brian. The reason that you and DREAM can do programming here safely is because I say so. These parents let their kids go on trips with you or even participate in DREAM because they know I'm looking out for them. So, if I decide that you can't do programming here anymore, or that it won't be safe for you anymore, it won't be. And when I say I'm still participating, that's just what it is."

Now I was really irritated—practically enraged. *Is Mecca out of his mind? Is he trying to threaten me?* We continued to stare at each other for a moment with a tense silence that you could cut with a knife. I knew I couldn't react how I wanted to, and I felt this could quickly escalate if I didn't pivot. More importantly, the DREAM kids and my interns could see us in the distance. I did not want them to witness any negative argument.

I finally broke the silence and said, "Look, Mecca, I know you, and I like you a lot. So, we don't need to have beef with each other, but you need to understand my perspective." I attempted to bring him along with me in my thought process. I continued, "I am responsible for these kids at DREAM from the city's standpoint. If something happens to one of them, the Philadelphia Housing Authority will blame me, not you, because I'm the director of DREAM." He nodded his head as I spoke and softened his body a bit. I continued to deescalate the situation and highlight the importance of the program and the children's safety to both of us.

After my words, his body language eased up a lot. He agreed that the program was good for the kids and that's why he always supported me. We chatted a bit more. Then he started sharing some ideas with me about other youth programming opportunities that he wanted to lead in the neighborhood. I told him I thought they were great ideas, and I reiterated that I just needed to keep DREAM safe, and it was not about him at all. He agreed and left the programming for that day.

From then on, we did not have any issues. However, I would often see Mecca gazing at me out of his apartment window in the Fairhill high-rise tower while I was with DREAM with some mixture of longing and perhaps even rage. What I was witnessing is not uncommon, in my experience. I was witnessing the frustration that comes from an adult, who like the children I was working with in the community, has lived a life that hasn't afforded them the resources to realize their dreams. As a result, when anyone comes in from outside the community and has, for whatever reason, the necessary experience or resources or leadership capacity to create opportunities, and is being lifted up as a change agent in the community, that is understandably frustrating to those who have longed to be that figure but have been so often thwarted by the system.

THE SECOND YEAR of DREAM was tough for me. During this year, I fully began to comprehend the hurdles our students faced. And it was a hard pill to swallow. The college road trip had energized our teens about the possibility of going to college. At the end of the summer, I even took Lewis to enroll in the Community College of Philadelphia because he asked me to. I was thrilled to demonstrate my support for him and his goals. He was our first "graduate" from DREAM, and now he was starting community college—which was everything we had envisioned. The other teens were enthusiastic about four-year universities that they hoped to attend. Some wanted to go to Boston University, Vermont Tech, or other schools we had visited. However, in the back of my mind, I knew the uphill battle the teens had to fight. Many of our teens in the program were in alternative educational situations, and some were reading on elementary school levels. It would be a rough road to get them through school and college. They now had a new vision for their futures, but I wondered, *Are we equipped at DREAM to give the support to make their vision a reality?*

I started to be more strategic in helping our DREAM students accomplish their aspirations. I set aside some additional funding in our budget to support a work-study program for undergraduate college students to tutor our teens. If this program worked well, we could expand it to our younger participants in addition to their mentorship. I hired four tutors to work with our teens across both sites. I was desperately trying to help the teens play catch-up for what they lacked academically. I believed the one-on-one tutoring attention could help. I even took on some tutoring myself. I met Malcolm, one of the teens at Westpark, at a local Dunkin' Donuts next to his housing unit from 6:30 to 8:30 P.M. twice a week to work with him on SAT prep. He expressed a desire to take the SAT but had no clue where to start.

Over the next few months, tutoring the teens was challenging, to say the least. The tutors often struggled to motivate the teens, and I had my challenges with motivating Malcolm. The teens' internal or intrinsic motivation was almost nonexistent when it came to academics. I would rack my brain to figure out why this was the case. I uncovered what I had initially suspected to be a key factor: our teens' encounters with teachers and the overall educational system had been horrible. To no one's surprise, the teens had endured some of the worst educational experiences that included being called names by their teachers, disregarded, and told they would not be successful.

Further, over the years, the school system had beaten them down—suspending and expelling them, making them feel like they did not belong, that there was no value in their education. It was the same story over and over again. The same stories my father told me, my uncles, aunts, cousins, friends, and fellow Black students had shared continuously. Now, looking at the DREAM kids, I was staring at the consequences of these experiences in the face. I wondered again, *Are we truly equipped to tackle this problem?*

The overall DREAM program was growing and taking roots in Philadelphia. We now had three well-established sites with over a hundred mentors and a hundred youth participants in DREAM. We had expanded the team at DREAM, and I now had two Ameri-Corps VISTAs supporting our programming efforts. We had made a name for ourselves in the city and were making partnerships across Philadelphia with other community-based organizations. We also acquired media attention from some of our corporate financial sponsors. Things were looking up for the organization, but, internally, I still was in turmoil about what impact we were really having. The mentorship was an excellent source of support for the kids, but the bleak realities that I witnessed these kids experience day in and day out were taking a toll on me, and I consistently felt like we were not doing enough. I continued to question, *What would be enough?*

By the end of my second year of DREAM, I had become disillusioned. I was unsure what, if anything, DREAM could really do to transform the lives of these children the way I truly desired. I was becoming restless with the task at hand. DREAM's programming model, resources, and infrastructure did not support the direction I wanted to go with the organization. Candidly, what I wanted to do went against the entire premise of DREAM. I loved the mentorship experience that DREAM introduced to the kids participating, but when it was all said and done, our mentors went back to their college campuses and the children went back to living in their housing projects. And worse, the children went back to experiencing dangerous, unstimulating school environments that made up many of the Philadelphia public schools daily—school environments that killed aspirations.

I deeply wanted to support student learning in a way that would allow them to better navigate the world. I was hungry to contribute to an educational environment that did "well" for kids like the mentees in DREAM, kids like my teens that I had grown to love so much. Were any schools doing this? Were there schools out there supporting the most under-resourced Black and Brown students in a way that was empowering them? Were there schools that created opportunities for children in these circumstances to grow and thrive? I began to ask these questions to those I knew. And everyone that I spoke with told me I should look into charter schools. I was not very familiar with the charter school model as they were nonexistent in my K–12 experience, but after some research, I decided a charter school was where I needed to go next.

Despite my feelings and plans to exit, DREAM continued to do well with supporters and funders. In the eyes of the public, we had our first "success" story with Lewis, our first enrolled college student—who made it clear that without DREAM, he would have never thought about college. In an effort to get more funding, we loved to talk about Lewis and his accomplishment. But was it true? In reality, I was losing touch with Lewis. His number had changed multiple times, which was not uncommon for the families and kids we worked with, but it was unusually hard to get in touch with him. His brother, Lamar, would attempt to update me with his number and what was going on with him, but he seemed a bit out of touch with Lewis, too. To make things worse, Amira and Amani told me they had heard Lewis was back "in the streets." I knew what that meant, and I hoped it was not true because Lewis had progressed so much. I also knew that Lewis had postponed starting classes though he enrolled in Community College of

Philadelphia months ago. And to my knowledge, he still was not going. I was constantly trying to get in touch with Lewis but failed in my attempts.

One day, Lamar told me that Lewis wanted to talk to me and asked if it would be okay if he came by the DREAM office. I was confused because, *of course, he could talk to me.* I had been trying to contact him for weeks or even months. I told Lamar, "Yes! Please have him come by!"

The next day I got a visit from Lewis. He seemed a bit nervous. His head was down, and he struggled to look at me. I picked up on his nervousness quickly and elevated the tone in my voice to show excitement in hopes of easing his uneasiness. I asked him how he'd been and what's been going on with him. He told me things were fine. He then went on to say that he thought I was "mad at him" because of his procrastination to start classes. Lewis then asked if he could still come around DREAM, maybe even if I could hire him on as an intern. I smiled at the wholesomeness of this interaction. I told him I was not mad at him but wanted to know how he was doing because I had not heard from him. I told him that he could come by anytime and that I was in his corner.

He said, "Thanks, Brian. I appreciate that."

I felt compelled to say more to him, and responded, "Lewis, I am not here to force you to do anything; I just want you to know that you have options. And to always remember that. You have unlimited options." Now I was looking at him in his eyes. I wanted him to sense my genuineness and feel my support.

He responded, "Yeah, you're right. I know I have options." He paused, contemplating my words, and then repeated, "Yeah, I have options," as if he were trying to convince himself that my words were true. Lewis then gave me a handshake that turned into a hug, and he left.

That was the last time I saw him.

What happens to a dream deferred?
Does it dry up

Like a raisin in the sun?
Or fester like a sore—
And then run?

In 1951, Langston Hughes penned these powerful words to describe his experience as a Black man navigating his aspirations in an American society dominated by Whiteness. When I contemplate my time in Philadelphia, I am often brought back to these words. I believe Cecil B. Moore, Westpark, and Fairhill Apartments were communities filled with thousands of deferred dreams. I feel that the dreams of the Black and Brown people living there, and in similar neighborhoods across America, are deferred, or rather, destroyed daily. They are destroyed first through the abysmal living conditions of the public housing environment that cultivates an animalistic, survival mentality. Then they are destroyed by the schools, schools that the children at DREAM would tell me they had no connection to, schools filled with staff that treated them with low expectations, schools that were violent, schools that were grossly under-resourced and never equipped to affirm who they were or to empower them.

As the program director of an organization named DREAM, an organization somewhat ironically meant to inspire dreams, I repeatedly experienced the consequences of dreams deferred and destroyed while in Philadelphia. I saw the consequences that Hughes described so brilliantly in his poem. I saw dreams "dry up like a raisin in the sun" and disappear altogether in the statements of the teen boys who believed they were fated to only two realities: becoming a garbage man or becoming a drug dealer. I saw dreams "fester like a sore and then run" in eighteen-year-old Lewis's internal turmoil that led him back to a life of criminal activity and drugs, a decision that inevitably made him run from me and run from his own aspiration to attend college. I experienced the "stink like rotten meat" that deferred dreams make in the literal stench of death and poverty within the PHA communities. I saw deferred dreams "crust and sugar over like a syrupy sweet" in the blank stares in the eyes of the children and their families—stares of defeat, stares of hopelessness. I witnessed the "sag and heavy load" of dreams deferred carried by the "street pharmacist," Mecca, that ultimately led to his anger and resentment toward a fellow Black man leading a youth organization in his neighborhood—something he aspired to do. And more than anything else, I saw those destroyed dreams explode in the ever-present violence, rage, and anger ravaging the communities and neighborhoods of Philadelphia. Despite all of this, I also saw moments of love and moments of joy like brief rain that would peek through the dark clouds of destroyed dreams. Love and joy that would create beautiful memories between DREAM staff, mentors, youth, and families.

However, when I think back to my time in Philadelphia, I realize what was so jarring for me was that I existed in a dreamless land, a land where the dreams and aspirations of young Black and Brown people were dying. And through witnessing the consequences of the constant crushing of dreams, I became disillusioned. I liken my cynicism to what many educators feel after years in our public education system, years working in a system where they witness and perpetuate the destruction of dreams. It's soul crushing. The problem seems too big, and its immensity brings on feelings of powerlessness. I would argue the chaos that was in the Philadelphia public school system at the time was partly because of immensity of the challenge. I would even suggest that the problem is not that teachers do not care, as some pundits like to say, but that educators deeply care, that they sometimes care too much, which makes working in the system unbearable. Therefore, in order to continue to work in the system some form of emotional disengagement is the only option. Sadly, I discovered in Philadelphia that I did not have the answers that I thought I did. I struggled to fight against an organization (DREAM) and a city (Philadelphia) that were trapped in a dismal paradigm. The paradigm felt impossible to break. I did not know yet that this was only foreshadowing a much more intractable problem as I moved through the educational system professionally, a challenge that I was only beginning to recognize. If Philadelphia felt impossible, what did that mean for the rest of the nation? I guess I would soon find out. But in the meantime, what about all of the Black and Brown kids? What happens to them?

All in all, my time in Philadelphia lit a fire within me to advocate for Americans to do more in this country to address the poverty that ravages our communities. We must create an education system that gives the tools necessary to raise those children, majority Black and Brown, out of poverty. And let me be clear, the solution does not mean creating schools that will lead students to score well on standardized tests, but rather creating schools that provide financial literacy and emotional literacy, critical thinking, and core skills that empower students to intellectually question their world and to become the leaders of tomorrow. We need to create schools that allow students to dream their way out of a dreamless land rather than discourage them and limit them to the status quo. The children and families in Philadelphia showed me that this vision is not only urgent but the lives of millions of students across America are dependent on us to make this transformation.

CHAPTER 8

The New Talented Tenth

The most important question in the world is, "Why is the child crying?"

—ALICE WALKER

FEBRUARY 10, 2016

I remember the meeting was on a Wednesday. My principal announced she needed to discuss important information with us after student dismissal. Such a request was not entirely unusual as Wednesdays were our weekly professional development days at Success Academy. I was still a new teacher, but by this time in the school year, I expected the intensity of full "test prep mode." I assumed we were about to be lectured regarding our perceived lack of urgency while preparing students for the upcoming New York State tests, despite all teachers being intensely focused on these assessments. I was wrong.

After the entire staff arrived, my principal shared that, once again, Success Academy was the subject of a negative press release. The *New York Times*, she informed us, would be releasing a concerning video which showed a Success Academy teacher berating a student; she wanted us to be aware before it became public. The media was "targeting" Success Academy again, she told us, as they had in October 2015 with the "Got to Go List" that had leaked. That report revealed the way Success Academy systematically pushes students out when they could not keep up with standards. She instructed staff not to answer any questions posed by reporters.

Like many of my fellow teachers, I was unfazed when I heard this revelation because Success Academy was not new to the press spotlight and media scrutiny, in part due to the political stature of Eva Moskowitz, the charter network's founder. I was curious what the video was going to show, and I even remember joking with other teachers that it probably was just a "normal day" in a classroom that outsiders were overreacting to.

That Friday, the *New York Times* released the video under the headline A MOMENTARY LAPSE OR ABUSIVE TEACHING? The video, recorded secretly by an assistant teacher, showed a first-grade teacher, a White woman, yelling at and harshly punishing a Black girl for not correctly explaining an answer in front of the class in the same way she had written on her paper. The teacher ripped up the student's paper in front of the class, threw it in the girl's direction. "Go to the calm-down chair and sit!" she demanded angrily. "There is nothing that infuriates me more than when you don't do what's on your paper." In the video, the child quickly scurries to the "calm-down chair" in the back of the room while the other students sit still, in silence.

As I watched the video, a feeling of uneasiness grew inside me. It's tempting, in hindsight, to distance myself from the harsh, "zero-tolerance" teaching tactics of Success Academy. How could a student so young be ridiculed and embarrassed for what seemed to be a minor mistake? But also, I was not completely surprised by what I saw. I had acted similarly with my students and had seen the same conduct, if not worse, in other classrooms. This type of teacher behavior was inherent in the Success Academy culture, as I was experiencing it at the time. I did think the teacher had overreacted, but only because the student was in first grade. At the time, I recognized her logic to "press" students to high standards, regardless of the cost. I cringe now at the thought that I was so unmoved by the video. I cringe when I remember I participated in similar behavior in my classroom. I cringe when I think of how one semester of teaching at Success Academy had desensitized me to the humanity of my own students.

———————

IN MY SEARCH for an organization after DREAM that had the resources and drive to alter education on a significant scale, I had landed at Success Academy in East Harlem. The more I bought into the performance-obsessed ethos of Success Academy, the more my students recognized my need for being the best. They would constantly worry about making good grades. Those concerns led to cheating and to students only caring about the "right" answer, regardless of if they understood the process they used to achieve the solution or the thinking that led them to new knowledge. This, in many ways, reminded me of my own obsession as a child when I wanted to succeed in school to draw a clear contrast between who I believed I was and my fear of meeting my father's fate.

This dynamic came to a head one day during the fall when one of my students, a quiet Black boy named Xavier, had finished his class assignment early with a significant amount of time left on the clock. As a rule, Success Academy insisted teachers ask students to review their work to confirm they arrived at the correct answer. We also would actively coach students and ask them to "explain their thinking" when we came to their desks. When I arrived at Xavier's desk, I looked at his math problem. He had the correct answer, and I was thrilled because Xavier often struggled with difficult word problems. I asked him if he understood. He smiled at me and nodded his head, trying to remain silent as others were working. I gave him a high five and asked him to explain his answer. He started to whisper his thinking to me, and as he was talking, I realized that he did not understand his answer or at least he could not articulate it. This angered me, as I had just had a discussion with the class about fully understanding their work. If the students were only writing down the correct answers without understanding, they would perform poorly when it "mattered" on the New York State exams. Irritably, I asked him again more loudly to explain how he got his answer. Now students next to him started to pay attention to our conversation. He could tell I was angry, and he nervously attempted to explain his answer, but he did not know how to.

At this point, based on the Success Academy training and modeling, I needed to make an example out of this student. I had seen senior leaders and veteran teachers go to extremes to guarantee their students knew "they meant business" when it came to academics. This kind of all-or-nothing attitude was encouraged and rarely received any backlash from administrators, fellow teachers, or parents. If I was going to lead my class to the top, I needed to do the same.

I angrily snatched the pencil out of his hand and began aggressively erasing all the work on his paper. Now the entire class was watching, and you could hear a pin drop in the classroom. As I was erasing, I said, "The thing I hate the most is when students pretend to know answers, but they don't!" My body towered over his as I stood over his desk. I then grabbed his paper, crumpled it, and threw it in the trash. All of the students' eyes were glued to me. I slammed another piece of paper down on Xavier's desk and told him loudly that he needed to redo the entire worksheet in the few minutes that were left on the timer. And if he did not finish within the amount of time, he would spend his recess and any other free time he had completing it until he could easily explain how he got his answer. The students were completely silent, staring at me. I then said, "If anyone wants to see me angry again, I dare you not be able to explain your answer to me! Now get back to work!" The class started vigorously writing. Xavier looked up at me with tears in his eyes, dropped his head, and began to redo his worksheet.

WHEN I CONTEMPLATE now how both students—my student and the first-grade student in the *Times*'s video—likely felt about themselves in that moment and how teachers at Success Academy, myself included, used authority in a manner that damaged student self-esteem, I feel heartbroken. What is even more heartbreaking is that I, a Black man, participated in damaging behavior toward students who looked like me for the sake of "achievement." For standardized test scores, of all things. Even though I can articulate that regret now, I was too deep in my environment to meaningfully consider my situation then. I was blindly following a school network and school leadership. My experience being observed, criticized, and corrected daily to become a better educator was a way of life. Harsh responses to the student behavior were normal because of the harsh treatment we received as teachers. What we as teachers were inflicting on the students was what was being inflicted on us. It became a cycle of toxic stress.

For at least two weeks, everyone I knew talked about the video that the *New York Times* leaked. It made national headlines and was aired on CBS news programs. My grandma Clara watches *CBS Morning News* religiously. After she saw the Success Academy video, she mentioned it to me on our weekly Sunday call. She told me she felt it was "crazy" that a teacher would "get that mad at a little child over something so minor." She was even more surprised when she found out the video was filmed at the same school system I was working for in New York City. As she said this, I interrupted: "That was not *my* school. It was just a school in the network. Our school is different; we don't act like that with our students." I was too ashamed to admit I had made a similar scene with one of my students.

She replied, "Well, I hope it's not your school because that's crazy and no little child should be treated like that. We wouldn't have let you be treated like that in school at that age. I wouldn't let none of my kids or grandkids be treated that way."

I listened silently and then agreed. After a few more minutes, I ended the call. The moment I hung up the phone, I felt crushed. My grandmother was right. No child should be treated that way. *What is wrong with me? How have I become okay with that sort of treatment?* I thought. *What is happening?*

AUGUST 3, 2015

"See, they need a strong male presence…that's what those boys need!"

The words still ring out in my memory. It was the summer of 2015. Success Academy Charter Schools, based in New York City, had hired me as a third-grade teaching fellow. As part of my training, I participated in a four-week "summer intensive." I attended along with at least one hundred newly hired Success Academy educators—mostly young, college-educated White women. The purpose of this intensive was to prepare us newbies with some additional behavior management skills before the start of the school year. Evidently, my presence had pleased a middle-aged Black woman, who I assumed was a staff member, standing in the distance as I was leading a group of Black and Latino students down the hall during my training period.

At the end of the training, my principal-to-be came to observe me. I was nervous. I had interacted with her only a couple of times in the weeks leading up to the observation, but this was to be the first time she saw me in action as a teacher. My principal was a young White woman in her late twenties. Prior to her career at Success Academy, she had been a management consultant. Our interactions had thus far been pleasant, and I appreciated her straightforward, no-bullshit personality. However, because of her frank and open nature, I knew if I did not perform well she would tell me bluntly, an awareness which heightened my nervousness.

Along with my principal, other senior leaders across the network watched us newly hired teachers and gave in-the-moment feedback. I was tasked with directing a group of third-grade students to walk silently down the hall in a straight line. They were to keep their hands by their sides while keeping their feet aligned with lines marked on the hallway floor, designated by color. I thought this seemed simple enough as I had experience with leading kids for the past two years in Philadelphia. That said, this level of structure did seem a bit intense for kids so young. Still, I was new to teaching so I relinquished whatever notion of behavior management I had to the "experts." Further, I knew it was showtime, and I was not going to bomb my first observation by my principal.

The group of senior leaders—all White except one young Black woman—watched as I moved the children down the hallway while giving instructions. As part of the training, they told us to encourage the behavior we wanted to see in the students by repeating the instructions. Repeating my "script," I nervously began saying, "Silently walking down the hall, one behind the other." But I forgot to tell the children to put their hands by their side. Standards for teachers and students were so high that this omission could be seen as a serious oversight.

Luckily for me, I had an ally—my newfound hero—a young Black assistant principal. From behind the group of White charter school leaders, she thrust her arms by her side in an exaggerated manner and made eye contact with me in an attempt to get my attention. Her efforts, literally behind the back of my new principal, jolted me and I quickly added "hands by your side" to my directions. The students moved their hands to the sides of their small frames as they marched silently. The senior leaders smiled in a pleased way as they observed. The young Black assistant principal gave me a thumbs-up.

Again, the middle-aged Black woman standing in the distance seemed to be impressed by how well the students responded to my directions. She remarked again that having a strong Black male presence was good for the kids and "what they needed." Her words felt comforting to me, at the moment. I was new to the world of teaching, and if my Blackness and maleness were going to be assets then I sure was going to take full advantage. Often, those intersected qualities had felt like liabilities.

After the students finished walking down the hall silently, my principal came up to me to give her review. "Mr. Fuller, you have a strong presence," she said. "The only thing I would say is that you can stand a little more confidently when you talk to the students. Let them feel your presence. Stand up tall and confident, and project your voice." I agreed with her feedback. I was a bit nervous with all those people watching. But I was glad that, overall, she approved of my performance. I felt relieved. I felt validated.

———————

SUCCESS ACADEMY CHARTER Schools launched its first school in Harlem, New York City, in 2006. The charter network was founded by Eva Moskowitz, a White, Jewish, and often-controversial former New York City Council member who had represented the prestigious Upper East Side neighborhood in Manhattan. Most recently, Donald Trump considered appointing her as Secretary of Education before she declined, and it was passed to Betsy DeVos.

The "Wall Street-backed" Success Academy, as touted by publications like *Bloomberg* and the *Wall Street Journal*, built a reputation by excelling on New York State tests with student demographics of all Black and Latino students—many of whom live below the poverty line. Success Academy boasts a 91 percent passing rate on state reading tests and a 98 percent passing rate on state math tests. These scores significantly surpass the public school district in New York City and other more affluent and wealthier communities across New York State. Students in the New York City public school system pass the state exams at rates of 47 percent for reading and 43 percent for math. In 2014, in New York City, 18.5 percent of Black students and 23.2 percent of Latino students were proficient on state math exams.

Success Academy's achievement at such a high level was unheard of and garnered national attention for the network and the founder. Schools like Success Academy were becoming more and more commonplace on the heels of the No Child Left Behind Act era initiated by the second Bush administration and during the Race to the TOP grant administered under President Obama. Through these federal policies, public education was becoming much more competitive as funding was tied to results—and Success Academy was determined to thrive.

Like many other charter networks before them, Success Academy takes a "no-excuses" approach to school policies and discipline. It is known for being highly punitive toward students—a reputation that the organization, in many ways, embraces. Often students are suspended for minor infractions and at relatively young ages. Eva Moskowitz states that these policies promote "order and civility in the classroom." Along with the network's reputation for being extreme in their practices, they garner more attention for being at the forefront of the political debate for parent choice in schools.

Growing up and attending public school in the South made me unfamiliar with the charter school debate. However, New York City was, and still is, an epicenter of the national dispute over whether charter schools help or hurt low-income communities of color. As with many political debates, it is an argument of resources. Public schools receive public funding with money tied to property taxes. Therefore, schools in impoverished areas struggle more financially. Charter schools, however, are both privately and publicly funded but privately run.

Additionally, when students leave a traditional public school to attend a charter school, they take the per-student federal funding with them, leaving the traditional public school less financially resourced but with the same overhead costs. Numerous neighborhood public schools lose money and enrollment as charter schools arrive in their communities. To many, the takeover of charter schools feels like another form of gentrification—destroying these communities' identity and sense of pride. Communities argue that charter schools leave neighborhood schools decimated with little to no resources, enrolled with the students discarded by the charters, and further stereotyped as "failing."

However, others in the same community think charter schools provide their children with the opportunities their traditional neighborhood school does not. Many families argue that their students do better academically, have more options, and are safer at the charter schools. For them, charter schools are a good source of competition for traditional public schools, pushing them to improve.

Like other charters nationally, Success Academy's founding premise is that they counter the failing schools within predominantly Black and Latino neighborhoods. Their presence is essential to provide a top-notch education to children who otherwise would not receive it. This mentality is the foundation of the policies, practices, and intensity at the school. Race also plays a significant role in the conversation. Like many urban traditional public schools, prominent charter schools are highly staffed and led by White teachers and administration while serving mostly an all-Black and Latino student body. Success Academy is no exception. As of January 2021, 75 percent of the network's senior leadership, 68 percent of its network employees, 62 percent of its principals, and 50 percent of its teachers were White. In comparison, only 7 percent of the students enrolled are White.

I was naïve about this political debate and the history of charter schools when I started working at Success Academy. I only knew I wanted to move to New York City and work in a school that seemed to prepare Black and Latino youth for a better future. My experiences in Philadelphia had angered me, and I felt that I needed to do more. I wanted to see a school that was moving the needle for the most historically underserved student populations. When I heard about Success Academy, I thought, *Finally, I hit the jackpot. A school that is producing excellent outcomes for Black and Latino students, providing them with options in life.* Looking at their website, going through their interview process, and seeing images of children who looked like me achieving academic excellence made my heart smile. I wanted to be a part of this network. I was ecstatic to get offered the job as a teaching fellow, and I would give it all that I had.

———

MY CO-TEACHER AT Success Academy was a Black woman with an Ivy League education who had previously worked in another well-known national charter school network—Knowledge Is Power Program, or KIPP. She was about seven years my senior and had more experience in teaching. And she was the associate leadership resident or an "understudy" of sorts to the assistant principal. I felt more at ease knowing I would teach with someone who had years of experience under her belt.

Our first task together was to set up our classroom. But what seemed at first like a fun, team task turned into an intense ordeal. Success Academy is extremely meticulous when it comes to how teachers assemble and arrange their classrooms, and neither I nor my co-teacher were familiar with these rigid expectations when it came to both order and urgency. It was taking us a lot longer to set up our classroom than the administration anticipated. The class library had to be ordered in a particular way, and the desks had to be in a specific alignment. There could only be Success Academy posters on the walls. All of these specifications were utterly foreign to my experienced co-teacher. Because of this, the newly hired assistant principal, a tall, light-skinned Black Morehouse man (also previously from the KIPP network), was in our classroom providing feedback. He complained we were moving too slow and needed to set up the classroom with more urgency. This was, I came to realize, a common theme at Success Academy. The assistant principal watched me methodically place books on our classroom bookshelf and was unhappy with my pace. He told me I needed to move faster.

I was a bit annoyed with his hovering, and I thought this was a menial request, so I acknowledged what he said but continued at my pace. My actions apparently aggravated him more, and he demanded my co-teacher set a timer. If I did not finish the task in twenty minutes, he said, there would be "consequences." I was infuriated by his controlling and micromanaging management style. *Am I a child to him? Is he out of his mind?* I thought. I was setting up my own classroom, and he dared to tell my colleague to time me as if I was incompetent. Out of indignation, I scoffed out loud at his suggestion; I laughed a bit at the ridiculous situation. I looked at my co-teacher and said, "Please, set the timer!" daring her to do it. She could tell I was irritated so she did not set the timer or acknowledge what the assistant principal said. *What is happening here?* I thought. My emotions had reverted to high school memories of dealing with condescending, dehumanizing teachers. I gathered myself and continued working in the classroom. *I am not even through week one,* I thought. *What am I getting myself into?*

AS A NEW teacher, I placed high expectations on myself on top of the extremely high expectations my network had for me. As with my job at DREAM in Philadelphia, I knew that my role in the classroom was one of the most critical positions I could have in society. But based on all the gossip from the veteran teachers about the school, I also knew this year would be challenging. According to the teachers and the statistics, our school had performed at the bottom of the network the previous year. Also, according to the same teachers, "the grades were poor, and the behaviors were out of control." The school had gone through three leader transitions within a single year. Before Success Academy hired me, our current principal was considered a "superstar" assistant principal in the network and was tapped to take over our school as principal halfway into the academic year. She had to take "extreme" measures to get things "under control." These rumors frightened me mainly because of the unruly "behaviors" of the students, as described by teachers. Supposedly, some behaviors were so "bad" they had an empty classroom dedicated for children to throw tantrums. Teachers told horror stories; they heard screams and banging coming from that room daily. Additionally, half of the incoming third graders were old enough to be in fourth or fifth grade but had been held back because of their "poor behaviors."

Among the third-grade staff, my co-teacher and I were initially seen as a strong duo. We were both Black and we both had previous experience working with youth. Because of her previous experience with KIPP schools and my reputation as a strong Black male with a background in community engagement, the principal initially placed many of the "behaviorally challenging" students in our classroom.

Data was a way of life at Success Academy, and prior to our students arriving, we received a data-filled roster of our classroom. This roster was unlike any I had seen; it broke down the students' academic performance and behavioral performance. The students were highlighted in green, yellow, or red, with green being proficient or positive and red being below average or negative. As I looked through our students' roster, I noticed that over half of our thirty-two students were in the "red" behavioral category. I also saw that over one-third of our students had been held back. From the start, this class community was daunting but exciting. I was glad the administration thought highly enough of us to place some of the most "difficult" students in our room.

The first week of school arrived, and I immediately loved my students. They all came in their bright orange-and-blue uniforms, wide-eyed, and ready to learn. The first few weeks of school were dedicated to establishing "systems and structures." There was little focus on academic content, barely any at all, and much more on behavior management and classroom procedures. Each day, we would run drills to establish robust systems and structures. The students practiced lining up in two lines designated by gender. They practiced sitting still on the rug with their backs straight and hands locked. They practiced transitioning from the carpet back to their desks quickly, quietly, and calmly. Teachers expected their students to complete each of these activities with excruciating speed and timed by a large clock displayed on the SMART Board. Success Academy founder Eva Moskowitz speaks about this practice in her book *Mission Possible*. "Fast is a religion for us at Success Academy. It's a core belief, our gospel. It's an operating principle. It frames almost everything we do." The sense of urgency was a crucial expectation for teachers. We would set the timer, give instructions, and then press start for every moment in the day. My co-teacher and I were trained to observe the students complete the task in a quick manner as if it were an experiment. We were collecting data on their level of compliance and speed. And if our "scholars" did not achieve the task in the timeframe, there would be a consequence. The majority of these drills—and they did feel militaristic—were observed by our principal, assistant principal, and various senior leaders across the network daily. There was constant, in-the-moment coaching for both myself and my co-teacher to ensure our class was "tight." The students generally knew these rules as many of them had been a part of the network since kindergarten or first grade. However, other students, especially newer students, challenged them.

One such student was Devin. He was a young Black student whom my principal did not promote to fourth grade because of his poor behavior during the previous year. I saw him as brilliant, charismatic, popular, a jokester, and extremely active. He reminded me of my first-grade classmate Eric, my father, and the other Black boys I felt so isolated from during my elementary school years. I felt an affinity for Devin from the start and wanted to see him succeed in my classroom.

My principal made it clear that he was "playing me" in one of her early observations. She told me I needed to be harsher and make sure he followed all teacher instructions at "100 percent" compliance. She said I naturally had the "don't-play-with-me" attitude when managing the class, and I needed to take Devin's lack of body restraint more seriously. The students at Success Academy had no autonomy over their bodies. Every movement was directed: where they looked, how they sat, where their feet were placed in the hallway, and how their hands were placed on their desk. Candidly, the only other time I had witnessed this level of body control was in the prison visitation room with my father, who, when coming to greet us, had to walk directly in front of the correction officer, hands by his side, until he was released to hug us but only for roughly ten seconds or the "CO" would intervene. Complete control of the students was a way of life at Success and the more "compliant" a classroom was the better the academic outcomes. Moskowitz calls this form of structure and discipline necessary as it "helps prepare students for the real world…prepare them for life's challenges."

In the second week of school, Devin was still "misbehaving"—not walking down the halls silently, not sitting still, speaking out of turn—which was causing issues in the class. Finally, one minor incident resulted in a one-day suspension by the assistant principal. When this happened, Devin's mother told senior leadership she was removing her son from Success Academy. She was fed up and no longer wanted to experience the same stress she faced during the last year. She also felt that her son needed to be in fourth grade.

The day after his suspension, I spoke with his mother regarding her plans to remove Devin from school. I had already begun to build rapport with her, and Devin was happy to have me as his teacher. In our conversation, I told her I disagreed with Devin leaving the network and I was sure her son would have a positive year with me as his teacher. He had some work to do to build his maturity, but I would fully support him in that growth. She was pleased with our conversation. She told me Devin had never had a Black male teacher before, and she could see I was having a positive impact on him already. She claimed his behaviors were significantly better than last year. I asked her to reconsider removing him from the school because I had her son's back. She agreed and had already set up a meeting to speak with the principal and assistant principal about her son's future at our school. The meeting was scheduled for the following week. She asked if I could please attend the meeting because she would feel more comfortable with me there, knowing that I would advocate for her son and could help her not be "bullied" by our senior leaders. I explained to her that the principal and assistant principal had no plans to "bully" her, but I would gladly be there to figure out how we could strategize to help Devin have a successful year. I talked with my principal about my conversation with Devin's mother and my desire to have him stay in the school. She listened and said that she looked forward to our collective conversation with his mother.

That weekend, I received a call from my principal saying that instead of reporting to our school in Harlem on Monday, I would instead report to another Success Academy school in Bed-Stuy, Brooklyn. I would work with the number-one-ranked (based on student performance on New York State exams and internal assessments) fourth-grade teacher in the Success Academy network. She told me that this would be a part of my professional development and that she saw potential in me. She felt spending a week with him would "set [me] up nicely." I was excited for the opportunity. I asked her about our meeting with Devin's mother, to which she responded that we would have the meeting when I returned.

I spent the next week co-teaching and learning in Bed-Stuy. The teacher, a Latino man, was animated, strict, and engaging. The first thing I noticed was how compliant his class was. He noticed everything, and the students were almost always adhering to the Success Academy standards. I was impressed by how academically engaged his students were and the rigor of their schoolwork. I was occasionally taken aback by how harsh he and the other teachers on his team were with the students, but he was, after all, the top-ranked teacher at the top-ranked school, so I figured he must be doing something right. My principal saw potential in me to be as effective as he was, so I tried to soak up everything he did and said like a sponge. The last day I was with him, I taught "shared text" in his class while he observed. This was a great opportunity as shared text was the Success Academy version of reading comprehension and writing instruction. Because some of the students came from families where English was not spoken as a first language, reading comprehension was a bit more challenging for teachers and students to master. Shared text and math were the focus of instruction at Success Academy and everything else was secondary. Similar to modern trends in schools across the country, Success Academy did not teach much history, social studies, or world events at the elementary level for the sake of doubling down on key content areas in preparation for the state exams. If students mastered reading comprehension and math, they mastered the state tests. Therefore, in my mind, if I received coaching from the strongest teacher in the network, my students had a better chance of excelling on the state exams.

At the end of the lesson, my mentor gave me glowing feedback. I felt elated. After dismissal that day, I looked at my cell phone and saw that I had a missed call from Devin's mother. I was planning to call her back but first I had a scheduled call with my principal to review my week in Bed-Stuy. When my principal called, she sounded excited. I gave her an update on my shadowing experience.

As we were getting off the phone, I mentioned that I saw a missed call from Devin's mother and asked if she had spoken with her that day. She paused for a moment. Then she told me that Devin's mother decided to remove him from the school in an earlier meeting that day. I was shocked and angry. I felt betrayed because, for one, we had agreed I would be a part of the meeting, and secondly, the meeting was for us to work together to make sure Devin would have a successful year. While trying to hide my emotions and uneasiness, I asked her about her decision to have the meeting. As a new teacher who was hoping to learn from her, I wanted to understand her thinking. She explained how Success Academy was "not for everyone" and that "there are thousands of students on the waiting list who want to be a part of the school so no need to fight to keep someone there who doesn't need or want to be." She went on. "This would be something I would learn over time," she told me while acknowledging my "good intentions." I was extremely bothered. Instead of speaking up in the moment, I said I understood and thanked her for calling. However, in my mind, I could not help but think that the purpose of this charter school was to provide a top-quality education for everyone because other schools were failing to do so. Maybe I was wrong, or maybe I just misunderstood.

After getting off the phone with my principal, I tried to call Devin's mother back. She did not answer.

———————

"MR. FULLER, ADAM SAID the effing N-word about you," my student Jada whispered in my ear just moments after the back half of my class line let out a big gasp and collective "oooooohhhhhhh" as Adam's face went beet red with anger. Jada and Juan had stepped off the line to tell me what happened. Juan confirmed Jada's report repeating the exact phrase. My heart sank. I was stunned that a seven-year-old White student would use such language in reference to me. And I was concerned that other students heard their only White classmate call their Black teacher the most racist slur in the English language. I thanked Jada and Juan for telling me and I directed them to get back in line. After the class was safely in PE, I instructed Adam to come and stand by me. As soon as I said his name, he burst into tears. He knew he was in trouble. Adam and I began to walk back upstairs to my classroom. The entire walk, he was hysterical, and I was silent. I was contemplating how I was going to use this as a teachable moment for my young student, who I cared deeply about regardless of his behavior.

I racked my brain, running over the prior moments to make sure I understood what happened. As I was transitioning my class to PE, Adam and a few other boys were chatting at the back of the line. I heard the noise and directed them to be silent. As we continued down the stairs, I heard a little snickering, so I calmly explained to the four chatty boys that they would miss the first ten minutes of soccer practice after school as a consequence. This angered all four boys because playing soccer was a central joy in their life, but this enraged Adam most of all.

A few months earlier, Adam had switched to our classroom from another teacher because our principal wanted him in a more "stable class condition" as he was a "good kid." I was pleased about this change because I wanted more diversity in our classroom. Truthfully, I was still stunned by how a public school could be almost entirely Black and Latino students. I could not believe that the schools I attended in the South were more integrated than schools in New York City. Adam was one of two White students in the entire school. His parents were upper middle-class and did not live in East Harlem, Washington Heights, or the Bronx like most of our students. They lived on the Upper West Side. Yet his parents believed deeply in Eva Moskowitz's vision, so they sent their child to Success Academy in Harlem.

When Adam entered my class, I noticed how comfortable he was when he chose to ignore instructions. Further, he questioned everything, which is a trait that I think is admirable but one that his Black and Latino classmates rarely exhibited. Anything that we did that he disagreed with or did not understand, he would question. This was odd to me because Adam had been a Success Academy student since he was in kindergarten. Most students who started their educational careers at Success Academy were well adjusted to the policies and procedures—no questioning the rules, just following them. However, as time went on, I realized that many of the teachers did not hold Adam accountable in the same way they did the other students. He was granted a strange default innocence that I rarely saw the other students receiving.

I even witnessed this dynamic in my classroom. When Adam jokingly stuck up his middle finger at my co-teacher and giggled, I suggested she correct him. I wanted her to know I supported her. She said to me, "Oh, it's Adam. He doesn't even know what that means; he's just copying from one of the other boys." Her reaction perplexed me. I disagreed with her and, using my best judgment, corrected Adam myself.

Adam was extremely intelligent; I might even say he was a genius for his age. Additionally, he was popular and liked by most of his Black and Latino peers. In many ways, he was the "ringleader" of whatever mischief third-grade boys would get into. There was rarely a time when Adam did not know what something meant. Frequently, with my co-teacher and with other teachers in the school, I noticed Adam would be the one who was granted a pardon subconsciously regardless of how egregious his behavior was. I was often shocked at Adam's behaviors, and his reaction to me anytime I would correct him. I felt like I was one of the few teachers, if not the only one, who held him to the same standard as his Black and Latino classmates.

Therefore, I was not surprised when Adam was angry with me when I impacted his full access to soccer practice. However, I was shocked at what his anger led him to say. Holding him accountable sent him into a racist rage that his mind could not comprehend. I suspect that the school environment had unknowingly created an atmosphere that acted as a powerful reinforcement for Adam's privilege in the world. What powerful reinforcement, if that was the case for Adam, was our school environment giving to our Black and Latino students about themselves?

When we got to my classroom, Adam and I spoke about what he said. I explained what the slur meant and why it was hurtful. He apologized, told me I was his favorite teacher, and he only used that word because he was mad at me, but he did not mean it. We hugged. Later, his parents cried. They insisted to me that they were not racist. I hugged them, too.

My principal suspended Adam for a couple of days, and the scandal was over. Though the storm calmed, I cannot help but think about other possible scenarios. What if I were never there to hold Adam accountable in the same way as his peers? Some days I wonder if he still is given passes or granted "innocence" regardless of his behaviors? His words, "fucking nigger" ring deep in my memory as those were the same alleged words that Travis McMichael said standing over Ahmaud Arbery, the young Black man from Georgia, whom he hunted and killed for running in his neighborhood in February of 2020. I am curious about how often Mr. McMichael's school environment acted as a powerful reinforcement of his privilege in the world. What passes was he given, and how often was innocence granted to him?

———————

IN MANY WAYS, it was true that Success Academy's Black and Latino students were pushed to be among the cream of the crop in their behavior and academics. Maybe, following the "Talented Tenth" theory W. E. B. Du Bois made famous over a century ago, those students passing through the Success Academy system would elevate their communities. The essential idea of Du Bois's flawed theory was that every race of people has an exceptional ten percent of people who can lead the race to glory. Our "scholars" were supposedly the ones proving that Black and Latino children can succeed in a White supremacist system, and it is the failure of the traditional schools, parents, teachers, and lazy students that was causing dismal results for everyone else. Similar to my experience of being representative of the roughly 10 percent of Black students in my honors classes, International Baccalaureate program, and predominantly White university, top charter networks represent that "tenth" of the success class of Black and Latino students in America's educational system.

But teaching students they are only valuable for their performance leads to absurdities that are hard to reconcile with the humanitarian purpose of education. I made a point to show off that our class was managed well. When we walked down the hall, our students were silent, but they also seemed like ghosts. When we had observations, I wanted our class to appear well-behaved and also to engage in rigorous discussion about our readings. There was plenty of performance; there was less joy and humanity. As I write those words, I have an internalized tension because part of me feels that Success Academy provided students with extremely fun experiences and a lot of love as well. I imagine this is part of the delusion that is Success Academy and other schools like it. The multiple atrocities in the school are soothed by the love, academic rigor, and connection that many teachers and students share with one another.

Our school shared a building with multiple New York City public schools. This caused tension in the building because the traditional public school's behavior management style was different from ours. The neighboring school's staff believed the Success Academy saw them as less-than. And the behavior of many of Success Academy teachers perpetuated this belief. Along with other staff members, I would verbally point out to students the difference in hallway behavior between a "Success Academy scholar" and a student from the traditional public school as we passed them. I intentionally cultivated an "us versus them" mindset. I would jokingly say to my class, "If I ever saw *my* students acting in such a way, they would have major problems." Though the students in the traditional public schools were often siblings, cousins, and friends to the students at Success Academy, they were different in our eyes because of the opportunity our "scholars" were afforded. They were the talented tenth. But at what cost?

―――――――

As I REFLECT on my time at Success Academy Charter Schools, the burning question in my mind is, "When was the moment?" At what point did I know that, as a Black man, I was actively participating in and upholding a school environment that was harmful to students who looked like me? Was it when I failed to be there to support Devin and his mother from feeling bullied out of the network? Or was it when I crushed Xavier's spirit in front of the class because of a grade? Or was it when I made mental excuses for the behaviors of my colleagues that I knew were harmful to students?

Or was it when I failed to speak up when I felt silenced? Was it when my grandmother called me to share her concern that I was teaching at a network where the teachers acted inappropriately with students over minor infractions? Perhaps the moment of realization happened when the only White male student in the school, who was subconsciously privileged so much in the environment, called me a nigger the minute I held him accountable.

Maybe a better question is, did the moment ever come? Was my need to be successful at my job too great to lead me to the moment of realization I needed? Was the "academic achievement" of my Black and Latino students as measured by the state standards too vital for me to come to terms with the harm I perpetuated? What are the human costs of being a part of the new talented tenth in our educational system? I know what it meant for me as a child: desperately trying to assimilate to a culture where my authentic self was undesirable and placing my worth only in my achievements. Were the costs the same for my students at Success Academy? And what did my example as their teacher show them? Du Bois wrote in *The Talented Tenth* that, "the negro race, like all other races, is going to be saved by its exceptional men." I am not quite convinced. I am not quite convinced that the Success Academy environment, or charter schools in general, develop such exceptional people, nor am I convinced that during my time there, I was one of them.

CHAPTER 9

I Don't Feel Safe with You

Don't you understand that the people who do this thing, who practice racism, are bereft? There is something distorted about the psyche.... And they should start thinking about what they can do about it. Take me out of it.

—TONI MORRISON, 1993

MARCH 5, 2018

I was sitting at my desk at the New York City Department of Education (DOE) headquarters, Tweed Courthouse, when a colleague announced that New York City Mayor Bill de Blasio had just named Richard Carranza as the new chancellor of New York City schools. I, along with my colleagues, anticipated this announcement because the man initially selected to become chancellor had backed out on live television—a chaotic fiasco for the city only four days earlier. Everyone around the office was clamoring about what had happened in the last few days and if the next person in line would be a right fit for the job. I had never experienced a chancellor transition within the DOE and was eager to see what it involved.

My boss, at the time, had survived multiple leadership transitions over the years. Her advice for success was to "continue to do good work for kids, and that work will speak for itself." I was aware that many changes took place during a chancellor transition: restructuring of the district, new deputy chancellor appointments, removal of old positions, and more. I was unsure how these transitions would impact the office I worked in, the Office of Leadership within the Division of Teaching and Learning, where I served as chief of staff—the only Black male chief of staff in the division. I was excited and nervous but interested in all that was happening within the NYC Department of Education. We were the largest district in the country, serving over 1.1 million students, so surely if I were to get firsthand experience of the politics involved with the transition of power within a major metropolitan school district, I would be learning at the most significant scale possible. *What would this transition mean for me, and what could I potentially accomplish within the organization?*

A few weeks passed, and the announcement came that Chancellor Carranza was making his first public address to staff, teachers, and administrators at the famed Stuyvesant High School in downtown Manhattan. Stuyvesant, at the time, was ranked the second-best high school in New York City. The high school is one of a few specialized secondary schools in the city where students must pass an entrance exam to gain admission. As a result, Stuyvesant is extremely racially segregated: roughly 73 percent of its student body is Asian American (predominantly East Asian), 19 percent White, 3 percent Latino, and a dismal 0.9 percent Black or African American. Stuyvesant was an interesting choice for the chancellor's team to make for his first public speech. I was excited to attend.

When I arrived, tons of teachers, administrators, and central staff members like myself were already in the audience. Everyone was anxiously anticipating what the chancellor would say in his first address. He had generated a buzz in the last few weeks by boldly speaking about equity in New York City schools. He was inspiring those, like myself, who wanted to use this platform to make significant changes for a school district that was notoriously segregated yet predominantly serving Black and Latino students.

Mayor de Blasio walked onstage in the auditorium to begin his introduction of the chancellor. He shared that, while making his decision, he knew he "needed someone who believed in equity at its core, who didn't believe things would be right until there was fairness and consistency throughout our whole school system." These words resonated with me and the rest of the crowd. After a lively introduction from the mayor, a short, charismatic, and likable Mexican American man stood behind the podium. The crowd applauded with excitement to welcome the New York City chancellor. I was thrilled to see the chancellor standing up there. I knew his parents emigrated from Mexico and did not attend college; I was inspired by how he reached the heights of being the chancellor of the largest school district in the country. His presence was comforting. He was like me, like many of those in the crowd that day, and like so many students of color who struggled through the current educational system.

The chancellor's speech was brief, energetic, and reassuring. His words at the end, though, stood out to me. As he was closing and thanking the mayor for his leadership with his equity and excellence agenda, he stated, "Together, we are going to take what you have already done, and we're going to put it on a stage that no one's ever seen." I interpreted those words as a powerful declaration that he would put equity at the forefront and New York City would be leading the nation in those efforts. I left that auditorium filled with excitement. I was young in the organization with a lot of potential. I was ecstatic to think that under this chancellor, we would be addressing the inequities in the school system boldly and unapologetically. This push toward equity was why I intended to work for the New York City Department of Education—to rally behind a dynamic leader who would genuinely advocate for the dismantling of the racial inequities that plague American education.

LARGE, URBAN SCHOOL districts are looked to as being on the cutting edge of education reform in America. Cities like Boston, New York, Chicago, Los Angeles, and San Francisco are consistently the subject of headlines about what is working in education and what they are doing to continue to advance educational equity. In my experience, these cities are always looking for ways to innovate and because of this, foundations, nonprofits, and other education-adjacent institutions are always willing to give money to these districts in hopes of setting a national standard for what it means to improve education for all children across the country.

I think there is without a doubt something to be learned from large, urban school districts. This notion was the leading factor that led me to work for the largest district in the country. I believe that when we dissect what is happening in these districts—the districts that are supposed to be cutting edge, innovative, and leading in educational equity at scale—we can further uncover the truths of our nation's education system.

JULY 2017

When I joined the New York City Department of Education, under the then chancellor Carmen Farina, I had just graduated from Harvard Graduate School of Education a month earlier in May. My time at Harvard could be best characterized as bitter-sweet. I loved the social connections that I made at the prestigious institution during my master's program, but most of my classes were underwhelming. I felt like the majority of the School of Education specialized in centering Whiteness and teaching White educators how to be better for Black and Brown children. Candidly, I thought that many classes in many ways perpetuated a White savior mentality—something that I expressed multiple times to my program leaders.

Although I had frustrations with the institution, my Harvard connections played a significant part in helping me land a role at the NYC Department of Education. I joined the department in the role of program manager on de Blasio's Community Schools Initiative. The initiative was founded in 2014 to promote the whole child approach. The schools supported "learning both inside and outside of the classroom and the child's family." At the time, there were about 260 community schools across the city. As program manager, I was responsible for fourteen of them—the majority of the schools being located in Staten Island and Brownsville, Brooklyn. The program managers had to ensure that the community schools implemented programming with fidelity, meaning all the wrap-around services (e.g., mental health, enrichment, restorative discipline practices, attendance support, adult learning courses, etc.) were functioning successfully. I was excited to join the initiative because I felt it married my multidimensional interests: community engagement, social-emotional learning, and rigorous academics. Additionally, most community schools were in the most under-resourced neighborhoods serving Black and Brown youth, which aligned with my values.

Coming from Success Academy, I experienced some culture shock the first time I entered one of the community schools. I saw children running through the halls, there was a lot of commotion, and they had more freedom than I was accustomed to at Success Academy. It was a stark contrast, and it was jarring, to say the least. I remember telling a Staten Island principal that his school seemed a bit "chaotic" as I walked down the hallways with him. Surprisingly, he did not get offended by my judgmental statement but instead agreed.

Over time I adapted to these schools and enjoyed visiting them often. However, the racial dynamics in the school were quickly on my radar. I was responsible for all community schools on Staten Island and would visit the borough at least twice a week. What I noticed immediately with these schools was that every school leader in Staten Island was White, though the majority of the students in the schools were Black and Brown. This racial contrast was vividly different from the rest of the city, which had a more diverse group of school leaders. And not only were these leaders on Staten Island all White, but many of them were also walking microaggressions. In meetings with me they would say shocking things about their students and families. I would hear comments such as "but we have a bunch of Mexican students here" in response to my probing about what the leadership team was doing to address severe disciplinary issues in their school. Or statements such as "these kids are the kids of those Black men standing around at the corner bodega. So, if their parents stand around all day and do nothing, what do you expect the kids to do? We're fighting a losing battle here."

These White, mostly Italian school principals, assistant principals, and other school leaders did not hold back in their conversations with me. What made it worse is often, these schools hired Black women as their "community school directors" to help coordinate efforts in their schools, but in my opinion silenced them and did not authentically value their input. Many community school directors began to complain to me about how they felt underappreciated and underused in the schools.

As a Black man, I was shocked and angered by what I heard and saw, but I understood that it was my job to support these schools. I was not going to let my emotions interfere with that mission. Learning to suppress my emotions for success in my career was something I was all too familiar with by this time. I could easily keep a poker face. I was frustrated that the schools chosen to be the exception in the system, schools that ostensibly promoted a more holistic approach to education, had leadership still stuck in deeply problematic and racist mindsets. While I struggled with the leaders on Staten Island, I did not experience the same issues with the leadership in the Brooklyn schools I supported. Refreshingly, they bought into the community school model. And despite the contrast of the two boroughs in their approach to their respective school environments, I built strong relationships with all the leaders. The Office of Community Schools leadership took notice and gave me more responsibility. I was thrilled. I was working for a high-profile initiative that I believed in and was contributing to its success in a tangible way.

In late September, roughly two months into my new role and a month into the school year, a seventeen-year-old Latino student fatally stabbed his fifteen-year-old Black classmate and critically wounded another at a school in the Bronx. This tragic event occurred during school hours in a school that shared a building with a community school. The incident sent shockwaves through the city and the district as this was the first in-school murder in over two decades in New York City, with the last one being in 1993. The seventeen-year-old was allegedly bullied consistently by the two victims and had even asked for help regarding the constant threats. As he was attempting to leave the classroom, one of the victims verbally attacked him and threw paper at him, which led to the assault. I felt sad for all parties involved. I understood the negative thoughts that being ostracized and bullied by classmates could cause. In elementary school, I too had ideations about stabbing my classmates who I felt targeted me. It was a dark reality but one I believe many students in similar situations face.

My colleagues and I in the Office of Community Schools were devastated. The murder brought national attention to the safety and security of New York City schools and, in many ways, made people question the student-centered, restorative justice approach that the Community Schools Initiative promoted. There was talk about needing more metal detectors in NYC schools and other "safety precautions" that should be implemented.

The need for more "order and civility" appeared very appealing for many after the incident. Quite a few of my colleagues worried how this need for order would impact students' school experience—especially our community schools that served the most underserved student populations. A few weeks after the stabbings, the conversations died down, and we continued our work in the Community Schools Initiative.

Over time, a leader in the NYC DOE who was the senior executive director of the Office of Leadership took notice. This office was responsible for the leadership pipeline in the DOE and oversaw principal coaching and development. The senior executive director sent me an email encouraging me to apply for her chief of staff role. I had never been a chief of staff before, but the position sounded intriguing, and the office seemed more aligned with my background. My master's degree from Harvard was in school leadership and development so it felt like the position could be a fit for my training.

Also, this role would be a more senior role within the district. Being a chief of staff overseeing a major office in the NYC DOE was a significant promotion. I was excited about the opportunity.

After multiple meetings with the senior executive director and the interview process, I was offered the role. I was elated. Besides the new title and responsibility, it was not lost on me that I was now making more money than most people in my family ever had. As I began the role, I felt extremely supported by the senior executive director and the rest of the leadership team in the office. They all wanted me to succeed. Also, this was the first time I had a White woman as a boss who was so authentically dedicated to advancing racial equity consciousness in herself and those around her. I was impressed by her. She was a Harvard-educated lawyer who was brilliant, thoughtful, and racially sensitive. It was surprising and refreshing. The office prioritized advancing racial equity consciousness of school leaders across the system—a system that had over 1,800 school principals. As a result, we as an office had a goal for each employee to participate in racial equity consciousness professional development.

One of the trainings we used was Glenn Singleton's *Courageous Conversations about Race,* run by Pacific Education Group. The training was a transformative experience for me. I even had the opportunity to attend their annual Courageous Conversations Summit in Philadelphia, discussing racial equity in education. The experience was informative and eye-opening. The summit introduced me to the work of racial and social justice scholar Robin DiAngelo and others who were renowned authors in racial equity. I likened this experience to my Race and Ethnic Relations course at Emory. The professional development opportunities provided in the Office of Leadership, alongside a dynamic leader, made me feel I was gaining additional armor in the battle for equity for all students—especially those Black students like me. I was overwhelmed with joy. After coming back from the Courageous Conversations Summit, I had the opportunity to lead racial equity workshops for the staff in our office, district leaders who coached and supported schools and principals.

Additionally, the senior executive director of the Office of Leadership asked me to organize and moderate an equity panel for the DOE. The event was a success and put me on the radar of other senior leaders, including Chancellor Farina's team. I felt challenged, and I was learning a lot in my role. However, there was still a part of me that wanted to have more impact and truly understand the complete inner workings of the largest school system in the country. The Office of Leadership was buried in the gigantic organization. We were one of many offices in one of many divisions. If I wanted to understand how to make impactful decisions in the system, I needed to think strategically about how to navigate the massive organization to get a better bird's-eye view.

OCTOBER 2018

I was leaving the gym on a Sunday afternoon when I saw an email from Chancellor Richard Carranza's deputy chief of staff saying that leadership would like to meet with me to speak about potential opportunities at the highest level of the organization. He asked if he could connect me to some leaders over email. I was on cloud nine when I saw this message. Chancellor Carmen Farina had retired, and Chancellor Richard Carranza had taken her place. Like with most chancellor changes at the DOE, the organization had already begun restructuring, and the fate of the Office of Leadership was in question. My current boss, the senior executive director of the office, was feeling a bit disillusioned and was in the process of leaving the DOE, so I had been somewhat uncertain about my fate moving forward. Therefore, when I got the email that leadership was interested in speaking with me, I could not have been happier.

Many of the leaders at this level of the organization had close ties to Mayor de Blasio. The person whom I was meeting with was one of the many White individuals who had worked in the mayor's office over the years and was now being strategically placed at the NYC DOE to help get things done. Leading up to our first meeting, I was nervous. As I think back over the years of my professional and personal life, I am not sure I experienced many instances of imposter syndrome. However, with this opportunity, I felt considerable doubt in myself. I was twenty-seven years old, and I was now going up for my second promotion in under two years of being at the DOE. Plus, working with a senior official in the country's largest school district within the country's largest city was a big deal—or at least I had made that determination in my mind. I was a long way from Sumter, a long way from visiting my father in the federal prison visitation room, and for the first time, I understood the magnitude of how far I had come.

Besides the imposter syndrome, there was something else I was navigating. By this time, I theoretically knew not to trust that educational systems, and those who uphold them, could actually move the needle for Black and Brown students. However, being a Black man, I still had a deep desire to succeed in these spaces that don't have an expectation that I succeed. It was a desire that I could not easily shake—though I understood the devastating consequences my need for success could cause. Being recognized by the top brass as a "rising star" in the DOE and moving through the system so quickly validated me in a visceral way. And I would later see how my need for this validation and my vision for Black kids like me would be at odds, often making me choose one over the other.

In my first meeting with this colleague, we discussed many topics. We talked about the chancellor's and mayor's vision for equity in schools, this co-worker's alignment with the chancellor's vision for equity, and my alignment with it. They shared with me that they wanted to counter the long history of not uplifting the voices of families and students in the most underserved communities in NYC. They emphasized how it was our job to "change the narrative" and "repair trust" in the NYC DOE for families. They were quick-witted, direct, and astute. I was impressed by what my more senior colleague was saying and slightly intimidated. But I did my best not to let them see it. I agreed with a lot of their statements. I believed they were on the same mission I was to truly move the needle for Black and Brown kids in the system, and I was excited to be a part of that with all of the new senior leadership.

After that meeting, I became chief of staff of a large division with over five hundred employees within the largest school district in America. In the new role, I would work with many senior leaders, including this impressive authority figure whom I had recently interacted with.

I was elated. In my excitement and curiosity, I looked up the other chiefs of staff and realized that I was the youngest of the "Big Chiefs," as I nicknamed us, and I was the only Black male chief of staff. Within the DOE, the chiefs of staff were the dynamic team behind the senior leadership of this immense organization. The chiefs of staff generally had a reputation as the people who "got shit done" in the system and knew the ins and outs. We made things happen and were the brains behind the operations. I was thrilled to start my new role. On my first day walking into the Senior Leadership room in Tweed Courthouse the tension was palpable. I saw the other chiefs of staff, and the energy felt like every person for themselves. Folks gave me a quick grin or nod, but everyone looked stressed and extremely busy. The mood, in many ways, reminded me of the "sense of urgency" energy that teachers often displayed at Success Academy. It was very different from my past roles in the Office of Community Schools and the Office of Leadership, but I thought *this must just come with the territory.*

One of the first events we were gearing up for was a community meeting to discuss charter school law and rezoning regulations with families. Senior executive directors were slated to speak. I was looking forward to this because I had already gone to a community town hall that involved the mayor, the chancellor, and other department leaders who were energetic and upbeat. This event was more low-key but required more preparation from me to support my division and our team. Showing my excitement for my new role and the work, the day before the event, I walked up to the desk of one of the White senior leaders to tell them how I envisioned our approach to the conversation with the families and what the "headline" of our message could be.

As I approached, they were texting on their phone. With eagerness, I said, "Excuse me, so I spoke with the community affairs team, and they said that for tomorrow it would be great if we covered—"

Before I could finish my sentence, they abruptly interjected, looked at me, and retorted, "What makes you think that what you have to say to me right now is more important than what I'm doing? You're making a huge assumption!"

I froze. I was stunned that someone would talk to me like that, and I was angered but knew I could not express it. I walked away from them and went back to my desk.

WORKING AS A chief of staff at this level was a steep learning curve. There was a lot of intrinsic knowledge about New York City and the NYC DOE that I felt everyone else had that I did not. I was still relatively new to the system and the city politics, and honestly, most people assumed I had the same level of background knowledge as the other chiefs of staff did. These assumptions only added to my imposter syndrome. Also, my relationship with my higher-ups was becoming more challenging by the week. I was convinced to take this role under the guise that I would be a true thought partner to the senior leaders in the largest school district in the country. I wanted to have a voice to help those Black and Brown children who made up most of New York City's 1.1 million students. However, I felt that most of what I did or said was questioned, doubted, undermined, or downright ignored. And what made it worse was when I was being spoken to, day in and day out, it was in a degrading and disrespectful way. Up until this point, I had felt very accomplished in my career, but now I was made to feel like I was inferior to everyone around me. It was like I was being gatekept out of the top of the organization after I was specifically asked to have a seat at the table.

Further, I was starting to wonder if I was placed in this position as a performative gesture to make leadership seem more tolerant and on the progressive side of the political spectrum. In my opinion, I feel some leadership reveled in the fact that I was one of two Black chiefs of staff, and I was the only Black male chief of staff. I believe they felt that it made leadership look good in the eyes of the public. Having a Black male proxy—a token, more or less—was a smart strategic move since we had to engage with some of the hottest topics and politically motivated aspects of the NYC DOE, many pertaining to issues of race and equity. I was intimately involved, by function of my role, with many of the issues that generally got the DOE in hot water with communities of color across the city. We oversaw school mergers, school closures, and district rezoning that addressed the lack of student integration. Additionally, we had an office within our division under a corrective action plan by the state of New York for not giving families of special needs children their proper right to due process. The DOE had historically neglected this office, and not surprisingly, the office had an almost entirely Black staff and a Black senior executive director.

One of my first tasks as the chief of staff was to make weekly visits to this office "to see what they were doing" because it seemed like "no one actually did work in that office," according to organizational gossip. Though I was not a COO, it seemed to me that much of leadership felt that it was better for me, as a Black person, to go over to the office in a disciplinary capacity to figure out what was going on. Of course, it was not presented to me this way, but that's what I felt was happening. It seemed like I was being used as protection because I was Black, and so if I criticized the office's performance, it prevented any racial allegations that could've been made. Despite whatever ill intentions senior leaders may or may not have had, I knew that I could form authentic relationships with the office staff to truly uncover the problem. So, I did. I also helped develop a system that got us in compliance with the state and helped restructure the office more efficiently.

Despite accomplishing everything I was being asked to do, I still received constant criticisms and beratement from certain leaders. I began to notice, these leaders acted this way with other employees, too. A special assistant (who now had become the one person I could trust on the team) and a COO whom I worked closely with also received criticisms and were spoken to rudely on a regular basis. Still, certain leaders' interactions with me felt more targeted. Sometimes leaders seemed so angry with me for unclear reasons. I honestly felt like they were trying to break my spirit—and it was working. One particular leader would go as far as speaking to me negatively in front of other colleagues within the DOE. My ability to fight back that I had used throughout my childhood when it came to toxic White adults who I felt were trying to undermine me had faded somewhat in my adulthood.

Further, this was different because I was now working a job tied to my livelihood. This scenario was not a school or university situation. I did not want to do anything rash that would get me fired. The typical confidence I had was also beginning to fade, and I was nervous to even speak up in meetings or give opinions because they were constantly being shut down or criticized. I could not believe this was what I signed up for. The more concerning aspect was that most of the senior leadership knew about this culture but did nothing about it. Knowing what I know now, I understand there was not much anyone could do. These leaders were a part of Mayor de Blasio's team, and the chancellor had to accept them whether he agreed or not. But as a result, I felt alone. I felt unaided on a dangerous island—where no one was looking out for me, and I was fighting to stay alive.

One Friday morning, a leader asked me to send an updated briefing to their inbox before a 10:00 A.M. meeting with the deputy mayor at City Hall. I had sent the briefing to them the day before. Still, for one reason or another, they had a habit of waiting until the last minute to send any feedback, which would generally stir everyone into a frenzy as they attempted to incorporate the changes with short notice. This morning was no different. As I walked out the door at 8:15 A.M. to catch the subway to work, this leader sent me updates to the document that needed to be changed before the 10:00 A.M. meeting. I decided to make the updates in my apartment because I knew the train ride would waste "precious time" and delay my ability to send the document to them. I made the updates precisely as they wanted and sent them back. I waited awhile to see if they had any response or additional changes before I got on the subway. I knew if I missed any of their messages during my forty-minute subway commute, they would be agitated. After about thirty minutes of no response, I was again about to leave for work. I was then sent a text stating that the leader had sent additional changes to my inbox and needed me to draft an email from them to the deputy mayor with the document in the body with the changes. I dropped everything again, prepared the email, and sent it to them. I then left to head to work because it was now almost 10:00 A.M. and I needed to be in the office for a meeting.

As the universe would have it, they made one slight change and asked me to resend it to them while I was on the train. I planned to send it when I got into the office before the meeting. This leader, in their impatience, sent me another text, ETA? which I felt was their way of letting me know I was taking too long. As soon as I was out of the subway and back in service, I sent the email and then texted them that I sent it with an explanation for the slight delay. My text seemed to upset them, and they responded, Ty. Do not waste my time or yours with explanations, it's not a good use of my attention . . . Don't use my attention for things that aren't about getting the work done. Esp when I am in a meeting and trying to get something done. As I read the text, I froze.

I was pissed. I was weeks into this role, and it seemed like nothing I did was good enough for leadership, and I did not appreciate how they were speaking to me as an employee. I was fed up. I was not about to have a White authority figure think they could just treat me like nothing and speak to me in such a demeaning way. I was responding to their every beck and call. I answered their text messages whether they came at 6:30 A.M. or 11:30 P.M., I accepted their constant criticisms, and I still put on a smile. But it seemed like whatever I did was not good enough. *This daily emotional rollercoaster has nothing to do with supporting Black and Brown children. Nothing to do with equity for all NYC students.* I had to say something. I needed to get my sense of power back. I was losing my sense of purpose.

I decided to ignore the text message and did not address them for the rest of the day. When I got home, I called my mother and aunt to tell them what had happened. They agreed that I had to handle the situation but to do it professionally. I decided an email was the best approach. In my email, I shared that I had some concerns about continuing to work at the NYC DOE. I went on to say that I felt leadership and I were "misaligned in our values" as they related to the role of the chief of staff and how people should be treated or spoken to. I made it clear that I give others respect because they are human beings, not because they are senior officials, and I would give anyone that same respect. However, I felt like some leaders only respected others based on titles and position. I ended the email by saying that my only goal was to serve the students in the system, and while doing that, I expected to be respected as a colleague. I went on to say that I would not stand for anything else. I was nervous about sending the email, but I knew it needed to be done.

In response, this leader requested a meeting to address what I said in the email, to be held first thing on Monday morning, at 8:30 A.M. I wanted to use this opportunity to help build a bridge between us. They had never asked me about myself or my background before, so I thought this would be an opportune moment to share more about myself in hopes that we could find a better understanding. I started the meeting by thanking them for their willingness to have the conversation and then went on to say that I hoped that we could move forward from this and build the best working relationship possible to accomplish exemplary work. I told them about growing up in South Carolina with an incarcerated parent and how that impacted how I viewed the world. I told them how I often felt the need to defend myself from discrimination from my teachers and White adults during my K–12 experience. I told them about the conflict with my eighth-grade principal and my high school IB teachers. I expressed that I wanted to share these experiences with this leader to help them understand why their interactions with me felt triggering and degrading. I told them that they had to consider the racial dynamics between us, especially if we were trying to bring equity and excellence to NYC schools. I was hoping that sharing more about my background and story would allow me to learn a bit more about them—potentially building a connection that I felt was missing.

After listening silently to all that I was saying, they thanked me for sharing. The leader also said that they had no idea about my upbringing and thanked me for my vulnerability. They then said since I shared, they would like to have the opportunity to share with me. These words brought on a brief sigh of relief. I was hoping to hear more about their background and what made them interact with people—especially me—in the way they had. But instead of sharing their background, the leader went on to tell me that my email "bothered them." They stated that the role of the chief of staff was to "protect" leadership, that is, to make sure they are politically safe and to have their back. But because I decided to send an email through our work account outlining my concerns, they could not trust me anymore. They specifically said, "I do not feel safe with you."

I was stunned. *How can this colleague say they do not feel safe with me when they are the one berating me daily and sending me negative text messages? How are they now making themselves the victim in this? So, when I decided to speak up about their egregious behaviors, I became a threat to them?* I was speechless. I felt like I was in the twilight zone. *How does any of this have anything to do with the 1.1 million students in the DOE? What does any of this have to do with serving the most underserved children we both want to help?* We ended the conversation with them agreeing that they would not speak to me negatively again moving forward, but I needed to decide if I wanted to stay at the DOE by the end of the week. They admitted to "being an asshole in their text message," and for that, they apologized.

What was I going to do? I needed this role. It was a good look for me to be this senior in the organization, and if I got past this slight hump maybe I would be able to do outstanding work for children across the system. Was I going to let this one White person stop me from accomplishing my goals and supporting Black and Brown children in the NYC schools? After this conversation, I realized that what I wanted to do was bigger than them, and they did not have the power to stop me. *I said my piece, and now they know to respect my boundaries. I will be able to make this work,* I thought. At that moment, though I decided to power through, I desperately was hoping my decision was the right one despite my misgivings.

———————

ONE OF THE most unfortunate aspects of Richard Carranza's tenure as chancellor of the NYC DOE was that it was filled with grandiose visions for change but just as grand if not more considerable amounts of controversy. And that controversy drastically impacted our experience at the senior level of the DOE. One thing that generated much controversy early on was Mayor de Blasio's proposal regarding New York City's infamous specialized high schools. Eight high schools across the city require a Specialized High Schools Admission Test (SHSAT) to screen for admissions. For these schools, the SHSAT is the sole factor for admissions. Because of this, the schools have historically been highly segregated, with only 10.5 percent admission rates for Black and Latino students in 2019, though Latino and Black students made up roughly 70 percent of the NYC DOE student population. The specialized high schools' student bodies were, and still are, majority Asian and White. The chancellor and mayor announced a proposal to remove the SHSAT testing as a requirement for entry into these eight elite high schools. With the removal of the test, admissions to these top schools would be granted to the top-performing students at every middle school across the city. Therefore, a top Black student at a middle school in the Bronx had just as much chance of getting into the schools as a White student at the top of their class at a middle school in Manhattan.

However, the removal of the test was not a simple fix. Three of the eight schools, Stuyvesant High School, Bronx High School of Science, and Brooklyn Technical High School, were written into the Hecht-Calandra Act in 1971, a state law mandating that specialized high schools' admissions test be the sole factor determining admission into these elite schools. The law, like the admissions test itself, had become controversial. Additionally, like the schools, this law was a way to act as a barrier to entry to the "best" public educational experience in the city or a more covert way to keep Black and Latino students out. Removal of the test would require a repeal of state law and a shift in the culture in the city (especially among wealthy families) as it related to entry into those elite high schools. The mayor's stance, which the chancellor supported, brought a lot of pushback from parents—specifically Asian and White parents, community members, and lawmakers. The chancellor was in for a tough ride, which made the atmosphere at Tweed intensify.

Along with the SHSAT efforts, there was a bigger push for school integration across the city. The chancellor took a "bold stance" on being more equitable across the system, and all of his deputies fell in line. In our division, we pushed a diversity rezoning plan for a district in Brooklyn (District Fifteen) to bring more integration between two economically different neighborhoods: a more affluent, Whiter Cobble Hill, and a lower-income, Latino Sunset Park. This rezoning plan would affect elementary schools also in the Carroll Gardens, Gowanus, and Red Hook neighborhoods in Brooklyn, all part of District Fifteen. The efforts garnered national attention and were the basis for the *New York Times* podcast *Nice White Parents* popularized during the COVID-19 pandemic in 2020. As the podcast pointed out, our challenge was that historically, White affluent families and the less affluent Black and Brown families were at odds about what an integration plan would mean for them and their children.

Our division was also launching a new-schools creation process, Imagine NYC Schools, redefining how we develop schools in New York City. Along with the deputy chancellor, I led the development of a design process that called for students, families, educators, and community members to create schools that were more responsive to their community needs. I worked tirelessly on this initiative: designing the overall budget, helping cultivate and secure funding through our philanthropic partners, designing the arc of the initiative, and acting as the deputy chancellor's right hand with this project. I was the internal face of Imagine NYC Schools, and, in many ways, I was the external liaison, too. I was happy to be granted this much responsibility. I was one of the driving forces behind a $32 million partnership between the city and big funders like the XQ Institute (run by Steve Jobs's widow, Laurene Powell Jobs, and the Obama administration's Russlynn Ali) and New York City's Robin Hood Foundation (at the time run by bestselling author Wes Moore, now the governor of Maryland). The launch of this initiative brought national attention because of the notable names involved and the more community-centered equitable approach to school creation that was innovative.

While the NYC DOE was sparking significant national racial equity discussions, I felt the racial equity we strived for was not happening behind the scenes in the department's internal workings. Instead, everything was merely a political game. I was experiencing deep feelings of being undervalued and overworked in my role. I had already established where I stood as it related to senior leadership's behavior toward me, but it did not improve our working relationship in any meaningful way. And as time went on, I saw how systematically the voices of Black people were being stifled. As the chief of staff of a division, though I was in my most prominent and senior role professionally, I felt the most powerless. And while I was feeling that my opinions, suggestions, and insights were being disregarded, I also witnessed this happening to other Black people, specifically some Black women.

Honestly, sometimes I perpetuated this toxic culture as well. I felt like I was being asked to constantly undermine the authority and expertise of some of the Black senior executive directors, only for me to be undermined by other leaders. Also, one leader's interactions with some Black women in our division became so intensely fraught that there were rumors and murmurs that they had a "negative bias against Black women." What saddened me even more was that the chancellor and his team seemed to know about the claims, including my own, but still did nothing about them. But candidly, as I mentioned before, I believe his hands were tied. A few White senior officials were placed in the NYC DOE by the mayor. And it seemed that they sometimes had more influence, power, and say than Chancellor Carranza himself.

Aside from these issues, I was experiencing daily cognitive dissonance as I was in communities talking with Black and Brown families through the Imagine NYC Schools initiative and the occasional District Fifteen integration community town halls. In these meetings, I was declaring that we, as the DOE, were hearing their concerns and we were going to be responsive to them. I was regurgitating the talking points that "this administration, this mayor, this chancellor were different," and we were lifting the voices of Black and Brown people and those generally disregarded by the system. However, as I was telling groups of Black and Brown people that the DOE heard their voices, I was living day in and day out as a Black person who felt his own voice was being stifled. How could I convince communities that we weren't just giving lip service to them when I as a Black man in a senior position within the DOE did not even feel like I had an authentic voice? *What was I doing?* I knew the truth. I was losing myself in this process, and I was losing my drive for why I was doing the work. Something had to change.

I REMEMBER THE day like it was yesterday. It was Sunday, March 15, 2020, and the mayor released an announcement that schools would be closing at least until April due to the rapid spread of the COVID-19 virus. Additionally, we staff received an internal email indicating that city employees were now allowed to work from home (those not deemed "essential workers"). The email was no surprise to me or other NYC DOE employees. We had been in preparation mode for this scenario for weeks. In actuality, the senior core team of my division, except me, had spent the entire weekend at Tweed Courthouse prior to the announcement as part of a COVID-19 working group. The district was rapidly preparing for the inevitable shutdown. Like most other weekends, I was on call and was responsive to emails and text messages but did not come to the office. I was now chief strategy officer of our division, a welcomed role change that had happened a few months prior, and our special assistant became the new chief of staff.

We had spent the weeks leading up to this point attempting to manage the chaos and uncertainty that was being brought on by the spreading COVID-19 virus. New York City was becoming a ghost town, and walking in a grocery store, riding the subway, and even being next to one another at work brought on additional anxiety. Everyone was on edge, and no one knew what to expect. The number of school closures due to COVID-19 outbreaks became unsustainable, and we knew that a system-wide shutdown was a sure eventuality. Each major division in the DOE had to work on specific aspects to help manage the impending closure. Our division was responsible for creating and developing the regional enrichment centers (RECs) that we as a district were required by law to have for the children of essential workers—roughly sixty thousand children. We essentially created a miniature school system within the larger school system for these children. And the school system had to uphold the guidelines of social distancing and all other COVID-19 CDC regulations. At this point, we did not know how we were going to do it, but it had to get done fast, as remote learning was scheduled to launch on March 23, and that was when the RECs needed to be ready.

After getting word that we could work remotely, I booked a plane ticket and flew down South to stay with my mother. I realize this was a privilege that many others were not afforded during this time, and I was thankful that I had a well-paying job that gave me the resources to leave New York so abruptly. My entire family had been worrying that I was in New York alone during what was the closest thing to an apocalyptic event we had seen in our lifetimes. However, I felt that leadership was initially upset that I had left. We had even argued about it that Friday prior to the Sunday announcement. It was suggested by one leader that I would be fired if I decided to work remotely—though I witnessed this same person encourage other employees to work remotely right after our conversation. I felt like this was another one of this person's tactics to upset me. I ignored their stance and let them know that I would work remotely as long as the city gave me that option.

The first week after the shutdown announcement was brutal. The pace of the work was excruciating. We worked what felt like twenty-four-hour days and through the weekend leading up to the start of remote learning and the launch of the regional enrichment centers on March 23. There was so much to do to create functional regional enrichment centers for the children of essential workers. Despite the issues I had within the system, none of that mattered because it was time for us collectively to work toward a common good. We had to make sure essential workers (mainly people of color) had a safe place to leave their children while they were on the front lines. And we did. The launch was a little rocky because many educators were still hesitant to be in buildings as there was national uncertainty of how this virus would impact us. Understandably, there was fear for their health and safety. But after the first few weeks of some hesitation from both families and educators, the RECs were running smoothly. Our division would host a call at the end of each day to check in with site directors to troubleshoot any issues, give necessary updates, and ensure they had the resources they needed. The RECs would later become "feeding site" locations for New Yorkers to pick up free meals around the city during the shutdown. The social experiment worked and became the basis for some early national evidence on the lower rates of the spread of COVID-19 in young children.

The most soul-crushing aspect of working at the NYC DOE during the onset of the COVID-19 pandemic was that we had no time to process the upheaval in the world around us. There was too much that had to be done to keep the system running, and I think this was our biggest flaw.

Quite honestly, I believe it's been the most apparent flaw of public education around the country. Though I was not physically in New York City, working from home and keeping up with business as usual as if our world was not turned upside down felt inhumane. And if it felt inhumane to me, I can only imagine how it felt to the students and the educators each day. Things had gone back to normal in the sense of the social and political dynamics of the DOE. And I was ready to exit.

Also, we were now in the midst of a burgeoning racial reckoning in our country, and I felt helpless. With the murders of Ahmaud Arbery, Breonna Taylor, and George Floyd, and the protests that followed, I innately knew that what I was doing was not where I needed to be. I believed the work of the DOE was missing the mark and generally creating more emotional trauma for the most vulnerable children—especially those Black and Brown children. I had to leave, and I had to find a way to address a major challenge present in our society. Now was the time. I had to put my talents to use. I had to write this book.

IN HER BOOK *White Fragility: Why It's So Hard for White People to Talk about Racism*, Robin DiAngelo states, "All systems of oppression are adaptive; they can withstand and adjust to challenges and still maintain inequality."

I believe this quote is a powerful representation of what I witnessed and participated in within the NYC DOE and is an explicit depiction of our nation's public education system. As I consider my time at the NYC DOE or being in one of our nation's largest systems of oppression, I see how the system can adapt and change with the times but still uphold and perpetuate incomprehensible inequalities. We said all the "right" buzzwords and even had the ability to call out the historical inequities of the system, but consistently continued to produce the same disparities we vowed to dismantle.

As I think of the NYC DOE as an organization, like all other educational districts across this country, I think of it as one that upholds oppression and a White supremacist culture. And when I say White supremacist culture, I do not mean to reduce it to "bad acting" White people, but rather a culture that has been well functioning for so long that it is now inherently perpetuating a racial caste system. And it became more apparent to me as I rose to the top of the organization. Further, I believe this White supremacy culture prevents the pockets of outstanding racial equity work that happens within the DOE from taking real roots and transforming the system, laws, and mindsets that perpetuate injustices.

Kenneth Jones and Tema Okun, in their publication, *Dismantling Racism: A Workbook for Social Change Groups*, outline thirteen characteristics of a White supremacy culture that they believe deeply damage an organization and inevitably help promote an oppressive and harmful mindset. I agree with their work, and I saw many manifestations of these characteristics during my time at the NYC DOE. I saw the damage that perfectionism caused when a senior official constantly critiqued my words and work products while expressing to me and others around them a sense that nothing was ever good enough. As a response, I chose to shut down in ways that stifled my creativity and contributions within the organization. I wonder if the same drive toward perfectionism causes similar reactions in our students. I saw the damage that our being in a constant state of urgency caused when it prevented thoughtful decision-making and instead pushed for quick fixes and visible results—leading to the disregard of communities and no real long-term solutions to those Black and Brown people that we vowed to serve. I saw how paternalism, or limiting decision-making to only a few in power, disillusioned us all—including Chancellor Richard Carranza. The final say always came from the mayor, and the team around him put in place to drive his agenda. Because of this, there was constant indecision, unclear decision-makers, and slow responses that inevitably further disenfranchised students and families. And sadly, a thoughtful visionary such as the chancellor felt an inability to drive any real change, which I believe led him to give up and eventually resign. And I understand this feeling because I felt similarly in my interactions with the organization.

And most importantly, I saw how the right to comfort and defensiveness by those in power threatened the ability of anyone to challenge the status quo or the harmful behaviors of "superiors." I saw this more broadly with the department's inclination to cater to parents who were uncomfortable with more integrated schools. Or how we accommodated elected officials, unions, and other influential forces even when sometimes it was in opposition to our vision for NYC students. And I personally experienced this with the senior official's declaration that they did not feel safe with me after I chose to speak out against their psychologically damaging behaviors. The NYC DOE protected the right to comfort of those in power so much so that they unintentionally created an environment that diminished the Black and Brown (both employees' and students') voices that felt the brunt of the system's power. And as I think more about the characteristics that I just outlined, perhaps silencing those voices was not unintentional but the entire point.

I should say that I believe this "silencing" is at the heart of how our American education system operates. And in my case, it wasn't just my email that made a senior official feel unsafe, but it was my authentic voice and my power. And more troublingly, I believe their response was a microcosm of the inherent fear of the American education system—a fear of the authentic voice and power of every Black and Brown child in this country. And this fear continues to breathe life into the White supremacist culture that severely disenfranchises those Black and Brown youth. Perhaps our American education system would *rather* have disenfranchisement than empowerment. So now, when I return to the words that the senior official said to me—"I don't feel safe with you"—I think about what they actually meant—and what that means for all people who dare to challenge the pervasive White supremacist culture that exists within our education system. Now I realize a more appropriate response from me to that statement would've been "You shouldn't."

CHAPTER 10

There's No Going Back to Normal

A teacher who is not free to teach is not a teacher.
—JAMES BALDWIN, 1971

ONE OF THE BIGGEST HEADLINES, if not *the* biggest one, about the state of education in the wake of the COVID-19 pandemic has been about the teacher turnover or mass "teacher exodus" in American public schools. All of the rhetoric about why teachers are leaving the system, the pointing of fingers, the blaming of students, or parents, or lack of district support, does not change the alarming fact that educators are leaving our schools at significant rates. The numbers are shocking. *ABC News* reported that thirty-nine states, the District of Columbia, and Puerto Rico, when surveyed, said that they were experiencing extreme teacher shortages in their schools. Over 50 percent of principals in America reported having a staffing issue in their school in 2021, as opposed to only 36 percent prior to the pandemic. According to Chalkbeat, a nonprofit news organization that covers education, "more teachers than usual exited the classroom after last school year [2021–2022]." At least three states have experienced the highest teaching turnovers they have seen in over a decade or more. The Government Accountability Office shared that between the years 2019 to 2021, roughly 233,000 teachers left the teaching force, about 7 percent of all teachers in the United States.

Although the teacher shortage has more frequently been in the headlines in recent years because of heightened media focus on the wide-ranging impacts of the pandemic, increased teacher turnover was a growing trend before 2020. In 2019, prior to the COVID-19 pandemic, the Economic Policy Institute released a report titled, "The Teacher Shortage Is Real, Large and Growing, and Worse than We Thought." This report highlighted that since 2013 there has been an educator shortage that has been growing substantially across the country. Not only were teachers leaving at a higher rate, but also it was becoming harder and harder to fill teacher vacancies. Like with all other societal issues, the pandemic exacerbated what was already happening in our education system.

I saw this firsthand as a staffer at New York City's Department of Education. The demands and challenges of the pandemic shed light on just how overworked and undervalued teachers already were. Though working in education during the pandemic was a challenge, I always remind myself I was not technically on the front lines in schools as a teacher or principal. I can only imagine how challenging that was. I can only begin to grasp the full systemic rupture through careful and empathetic listening to the education professionals I worked with or who told me their stories. I believe to understand why we are losing teachers at such alarming rates, we must understand what happened with them in our schools during the pandemic. And as we uncover that authentic story, most important for me are the following questions: What role has the undercurrent of racism and White supremacy in the American education system played in the challenges teachers faced and are continuing to face in the aftermath of COVID-19? And maybe most relevant of all: How is the mass teacher shortage impacting our students, especially Black and marginalized learners?

———

MARCH 12, 2020

"Whew, I am glad the school ended up closing. Being remote for a week will give me a breather" was the thought that ran through my aunt Tajuana's mind on that Thursday evening in early March of 2020 when her high-performing public school district in Georgia announced a week of "digital learning" for all students across the district. She, an elementary school teacher with twelve years of experience, was already feeling exhausted and overworked by this point in the school year. She was teaching third grade at a Title I school, meaning the school had a high percentage of low-income students, mostly Latino students with a smaller percentage of Black students. The majority of those enrolled at the school were English language learners. The district had put a tremendous amount of pressure on the school to succeed. Her third-graders would be taking the Georgia state standardized test in April and the spring semester was already picking up pace. In her mind, these few days of digital learning were what she and her students needed as a "nice reset."

Prior to the announcement, her school had already asked all teachers to prepare three days' worth of lessons and upload them to a digital platform—eCLASS. The district had already developed an online platform for students and teachers years before the pandemic happened. My aunt Tajuana thought the transition to digital learning would be fairly easy for these few days. Further, she was not too familiar with the "novel coronavirus" and thought that school could not possibly be closed for more than a week. Some of her colleagues were more invested in the news coverage of COVID-19 and so they were more concerned, but still most of the teachers she interacted with thought that this would be a quick passing "virus" and things would be back to normal in no time.

Well, as we all know, things did not "go back to normal." One week of digital learning turned into two weeks, two turned into three, which eventually turned into a digital learning model for the remainder of the academic year. The once welcomed "vacation" slowly turned into a nightmare. Even in the first week, my aunt realized things would be more challenging than originally expected. The switch to digital learning did not go as smoothly as initially planned. Many parents and students were not as familiar with the eCLASS platform as the school had hoped. They only had ever used the system a couple of times and in those instances, it had been presented as a way to supplement in-person instruction but never as a way to replace it. Now that online instruction was the only form of learning, all the challenges of onboarding to the new platform were revealed.

First, the students who had access to a computer at home were extremely confused about how to use the learning platform. This translated to parents and families calling and texting teachers, including my aunt and her colleagues, all throughout the day and evening, significantly past school operating hours. My aunt described this sudden expansion of the workday as extremely draining. Then there were students who did not have any computer access at home or the students who simply did not participate. According to my aunt, roughly 60 percent of the students in her classroom did not show up for class at all for the first few weeks of digital learning. This was not unique to her; her colleagues across the district experienced the same phenomenon. Similarly, in NYC, I was observing the same levels of absenteeism in my role at the DOE. We were getting consistent information from principals and superintendents across the city that many students were just not showing up at all to remote learning, which was causing significant stress on teachers who were still being held "accountable" for the students.

Everyone was winging it. Chaos became the new norm and my aunt and her colleagues were attempting to do their best in their newfound reality. But despite the extended work hours, unprecedented expectations, and the pervasive feeling of uncertainty, one positive aspect of the situation was that the teachers and administrators had a sense of solidarity, of "we're all in this together." My aunt and her fellow teachers were all navigating uncharted territory together at first and that made the work more bearable. However, the feelings of comradery soon shifted.

Like all other school districts across the country, my aunt's district realized that remote learning was not going away anytime soon. This way of providing instruction was the new normal and they would now be held accountable for the learning of their students within this changed landscape. With that in mind, the Georgia district purchased access to Zoom and mandated its use in all schools, and provided a laptop device to every student to ensure attendance and participation. New expectations for the teachers also came with the new technology at a dizzying and unforgiving pace. It did not matter if teachers were unfamiliar with Zoom technology, were uncertain because they had never taught online before, or had no training or time to prepare. They had to figure it out quickly and without meaningful support. And they were still being held accountable for the quality of their lessons and the performance of their students. My aunt, when recalling this time, said just when she "thought teaching couldn't get any more stressful, any worse, it did." Administrators from all across the district could now "pop in" to the teacher's Zoom classroom unannounced to observe lessons and critique the teacher's performance. However, according to my aunt, the administrators were completely at a loss as well. This was the most unsettling change for her and her fellow colleagues. The school principal and assistant principals could not truly give guidance because they did not know what to do. Yet these same administrators and others across the district were holding the teachers accountable for lessons and student performance. It was bizarre and left the teachers feeling confused and completely unsupported. Everyone was winging it.

The change in expectations for teachers changed the environment from collaborative to competitive, and administrators manipulated this competitive environment in hopes of fueling better performance. Virtual staff meetings were now filled with administrators publicly highlighting some teachers' virtual lessons while disparaging others. It became a dog-eat-dog environment much worse than in the pre-pandemic era. Ironically, though expectations were skyrocketing for teachers, they were plummeting for students. My aunt reflects that one of the hardest aspects of virtual learning was forcing teachers to lower their expectations for students. Teachers were made to feel that they essentially had to pass students even if the students were not doing any work or showing up to virtual class. No learning, no growth, just moving them through the system. This lowering of standards for a twelve-year Black teacher who dedicated herself and her entire career to serving Black and Brown students and pushing them toward excellence was devastating and felt unethical in ways that are hard to express. The system was failing the students more than ever and now she was forced to be a part of the problem. Yes, these students needed grace and understanding, but they did not need to be passed through the system without much learning just to prevent the state from deeming the school or district as underperforming. The damage to students that my aunt felt like she was participating in and the lack of support and respect she was receiving were becoming unbearable. Time went by and within a year her entire grade team had either left the school or quit teaching altogether. She was the only one left. Was she next? She deeply loved her job and the kids. But this all was too much for any person to bear. She knew something had to change. Even if that something meant leaving the classroom for good.

AS I HAVE highlighted throughout this book, a person's race consistently plays a role in how they receive education in this country and is underneath what is inherently flawed within our education system. That fact is no different when it comes to the teacher turnover and post-pandemic teacher shortage that we are currently facing. Predominantly Black and Latino, low-income urban and rural school districts have the highest rates of teacher turnover as well as teacher shortages. According to a 2022 US Department of Education survey, high-needs districts report having a much higher percentage of teacher vacancies than schools with Whiter, wealthier student populations. And even prior to the pandemic, high-poverty schools had twice the rate of teacher turnover than lower- to medium-poverty schools across the country, the National Center for Education Statistics reported.

These stats only add to the current inequitable conditions in our public schools that, as of 2023, have the largest academic performance gap between Black and White students since 1978. The data is staggering. We are not moving forward, we are regressing. And our teachers are at a crossroads, especially those teachers in high-needs communities. How can they continue to go on in an educational system that does not value a large subset of students (those Black and marginalized) and also undervalues them as educators? This question is one that millions of educators across the nation are struggling with, even the most dedicated and tenured educators out there. Even educators like my grandfather, who after serving twenty-six years in the US military, as of 2023, is in his thirtieth year as a ninth-grade JROTC high school teacher in rural South Carolina.

AUGUST 2020

It was the start of the school year after COVID-19 shut down schools across the nation and my grandfather's school district had announced they would be starting the academic year "fully remote." At the time, my grandfather did not know what to expect as he was not very familiar with virtual learning. The previous spring, when Governor McMaster of South Carolina announced on March 16th that all South Carolina schools would be remote for a month and would be back open "by Easter" (echoing the then President Donald Trump's sentiments), my grandfather prepared a seventy-five-page booklet with the JROTC curriculum for his students to take home in order to complete the rest of the work for the semester. The packet had all the assignments the students needed until the end of the school year, and he decided he would assign work out of the pamphlet and ask students to email him the answers. During this time, my grandfather would still go to the school so students and parents could stop by to ask any question they may have had during the initial school shutdown. This arrangement worked well for him and his students.

Now, the school was forcing everyone to participate in virtual learning starting this new academic year, and my grandfather, who was not as technologically savvy as he felt he needed to be, was worried about how this would impact his teaching. Like most everywhere else in the nation, the initial start of fully virtual learning for his school was chaotic. Teachers were mandated to take attendance in the morning when many students did not show up or were having Wi-Fi or device connectivity issues. This was extremely frustrating for my seventy-four-year-old grandfather. What made it worse was that once students received their school-issued Chromebooks, they realized that the only thing they had to do was sign on for attendance roll call, then log off afterward. Because of the remote learning, attendance became a big part of a student's grade, but the students would find a way to "game" the system because they knew the teachers "had to pass them." My grandfather was not tolerating this behavior in his class and understood the importance of students attending class and learning. Therefore, he would do roll calls randomly throughout the class time, not just in the beginning, and often many students would not be present, so he would mark them absent. After the first quarter of the school year, when his assistant principal saw that attendance was extremely low in my grandfather's class, he was asked to explain why. My grandfather shared that the students were not showing up for the entire class, so he would mark them absent, but to his surprise his assistant principal told him that he needed to count the students present in class, regardless if they only showed up for the first two minutes of the class time. He knew how damaging this was for the students' future and was frustrated that he was being compromised in this way. He had never seen anything like this in his almost thirty years of teaching.

By the middle of the school year the district had determined that they would switch to a hybrid model of teaching. Roughly four to five students would be in person in each class while the remainder would be on Zoom. This made teaching even more difficult because often the students who were in the class could understand what was happening but the ones who were on Zoom would be confused. Also, given the demographics of the school (rural, extremely impoverished, a mostly Black community), many of the high schoolers who were supposed to be learning at home became caretakers for their little siblings when the parents went to work. Therefore, the students who were on Zoom would often get distracted by the quarrels or needs of their younger siblings and if their microphones were unmuted it would distract the entire class, both the virtual students and the in-person students. And aside from being caretakers for their siblings, many students were caretakers for an elderly relative and their lessons would often be interrupted by this responsibility as well. For my grandfather, this mode of teaching was not sustainable, and he vowed that if teaching would not return to in person by the next school year, this would be his last year in the classroom. In his words, real education was built on strong relationships and face-to-face interaction. Without those elements, it was no longer worth it—it was too damaging to him and his students.

YOUNGER, LESS EXPERIENCED teachers grappled with the same challenges that more veteran teachers did during the transition to virtual learning, and in some instances to an even greater degree. A friend of mine was reentering the classroom in the fall of 2020 with only one year of prior teaching experience. Peter hoped that returning to the classroom when America most needed teachers would be the right thing to do to support students. The predominantly Somali American public charter school in Minneapolis, Minnesota, he taught at was set to be fully virtual to begin the year; therefore he would be starting as a new high school English teacher without the opportunity to meet his students in person.

Like in my aunt's, grandfather's, and most of the nation's situation, the initial virtual learning environment was turbulent and filled with uncertainty. Peter felt that "the only reality that was consistent from day to day was chaos and lack of clarity." What made

matters worse was how extremely challenging it was to build relationships as a new teacher when all interactions were virtual. He,
one of the roughly eighty thousand new teachers hired every year,
was entering a school environment where it was nearly impossible
to be set up for success. Though not unattainable, it was extremely
labor-intensive to build authentic relationships with his high
school students who, before the pandemic, were already prone to
be rightfully skeptical, confused, and a bit checked out about the
value of the education system, but now had every reason to reject
the arbitrary requirements and low expectations being pitched to
them. High schoolers are extremely adept at detecting frivolous or
inconsistent policies. As in my aunt's case, there was a lack of use-
ful guidance from administration as they were also overwhelmed,
and expectations in general were changing almost weekly. And,
like for my aunt, the workday often lingered late into the evenings
and the weekends in order to keep up with the demands of adapt-
ing curriculum for online learning, technology troubleshooting,
and being available to support students and families with academic and emotional needs. Furthermore, his high school students
were understandably disengaged from the school process because
they had other priorities now that they were present in their
homes every day. Those priorities included being caretakers for
their younger siblings and families or working jobs to help their
families get by, similar to what my grandfather experienced in his
rural South Carolina school community.

Predictably, my friend's stress turned to burnout which eventually led to an honest questioning of his own stamina and ability
to carry on. Maybe he had made the wrong decision to go back into
the classroom. Maybe his talents weren't best utilized in schools.
Maybe he needed to take a break from teaching and return when
he could truly be effective. Maybe the post-pandemic education
system was too damaged, and students were too disengaged for
him to be able to ever be successful as an educator. Maybe he was
enabling more damage to his students and to himself than progress
and learning. Maybe the new normal was something that he could
never get used to. Before the pandemic, 44 percent of teachers left

the profession within five years. For those teachers who started teaching during the pandemic like Peter, the probability and reality of leaving teaching felt higher and higher.

———————

ACCORDING TO THE *Wall Street Journal*, at least three hundred thousand public school teachers and other school-based staff left the field between February 2020 and May 2022. My aunt Tajuana was one of those public school teachers and so was my friend Peter. When asking those teachers closest to me what is the reason that so many educators are leaving the workforce, I consistently get the same answers: lack of student accountability and discipline, being overworked and underpaid (teachers make 23.5 percent less than other Americans with similar professional credentials), feelings of being unsafe in schools (from mass shootings and COVID-19), lack of respect and support from administrators, and finally a realization from many teachers that their talents will be respected elsewhere if not in the public school system. These all align with articles and studies that have been reporting on the phenomenon in recent years. Teachers have received so much scrutiny: whether it was the general public complaining that all students needed to go back to school regardless if it was jeopardizing the health of teachers, or being thrown into a political war over what can be taught in our schools about our racial history in America, or being blamed for all the challenges that children are facing in a post-pandemic society, teachers are without a doubt overwhelmed by the state of education right now and clearly are not standing for it any longer.

So how do we fix a problem that many are projecting will get worse in the coming years? What is our solution? I think we must move past the surface of the issue that our public schools are facing and address what's been lying dormant underneath. All of the elements I have mentioned thus far as factors contributing to the teacher shortage are well known and well reported.

But what many folks are not talking about is what I would say is the matter at the heart of this book. American public schools for over a century have been perpetrators of violence, misinformation, and the destruction of dreams for millions of children in this country. We have become so consumed by funding, state standards, and rote learning that students, especially Black and other marginalized students, are not allowed to be fully human and explore their creativity and critical thinking skills in a healthy way. And, in that process, teachers have become manipulated pawns. How inhumane was it for a national school system to teach students as normal when a world crisis was unfolding right before our eyes? For teachers and students alike, there was no acknowledgment of their humanity, their mental health, who they were, and what they were facing during the COVID-19 crisis. I believe one of the things the pandemic has done is open the eyes of many students and educators to a crisis that has already been building for years in our education system. We are not free to think, to teach, to learn, but rather forced to fall into a White supremacist model of an education system that blatantly disregards a significant subset of its students and treats its teachers like disposable machines.

Often throughout the pandemic, I would hear the phrase "there is no going back to normal" in regard to our education system. And I fully agree with that statement. What the pandemic has uncovered for all of us connected to education is the bleak picture of what our education system has become and, in my candid opinion, what it has always been. We have a system that has never truly honored our students, our teachers, and has actively harmed those most marginalized. So, there is no going back to normal now, especially as more of us awaken to our public education's ugly truth. There is a demand, as shown by students and educators, for something more meaningful, something inspiring, something more humane in our system. And if our nation does not answer that demand, and actively transform our education system for the better, then we are witnessing the disintegration of an American education system as we know it. And thus, a disintegration of America.

CHAPTER 11

I Am Enough

What white people have to do is try to find in their own hearts why it was necessary to have a nigger in the first place.... But if you think I'm a nigger, it means you need it.... [And] you've got to find out why. And the future of the country depends on that.

—JAMES BALDWIN, 1963

APRIL 15, 2021

I was sitting on my living room couch on the Upper West Side of Manhattan when I suddenly saw the charcoal-colored smoke billowing from under the door of my living room coat closet. My friend and former Harvard classmate and I jumped up to see what was happening. I ran to open the closet door, and as I opened it, the oxygen from the room added fuel to an already blazing fire. As I stood in the closet doorway, flames from the fire jumped out and nicked the back of my hand, administering second-degree burns. I had never been in a house fire before, so I was stunned. Luckily, my friend was there with me, and an innate survival instinct sprang us both into action.

Only a few short hours earlier, I had finished a final-round interview for a chief strategy officer role at a national educational consulting firm that had a heavy focus on using data and test scores to support "closing the achievement gap for Black and Brown children." Additionally, this organization was led by many former business consulting "experts" from McKinsey & Company and similar top business consulting firms. The organization prided itself on its "rigorous, objective" hiring process. But, if I'm honest, there were a few red flags during the interview process, one of which was that many of the organizational leaders had come from an industry that historically has been racially tone-deaf—management consulting. The two additional red flags that were especially apparent were their partnerships with problematic charter schools (networks similar to Success Academy) and their inability to speak confidently about their internal organizational racial equity work when I asked. However, I overlooked these qualities for the time being and bent over backward in my attempts to secure a role in their organization. Despite my best efforts and weeks of hard work, I knew I had bombed the final interview. The extensive time I had invested was in vain. When they told me I was not the "right fit," I was devastated. Even when I also knew deep down the role was not for me, my need to "win" was still present, and still hard for me to shake. My internal desire to achieve was still appeased by validation from organizations like these, educational organizations considered "rigorous" and results oriented.

So, I was already having a pretty bad day, and now the fire spreading through my living room was the icing on an already disastrous cake. At this point, the smoke had engulfed my apartment, and the fire was getting progressively worse. I ran to grab some flour to throw on the fire in an attempt to suffocate the flames (I do not recommend this!). I dumped a whole bag on the flames while my friend sprinted to grab pitchers of water. As we began throwing water on the fire, I called 911 and opened my windows in what felt like sixty seconds. I was moving at rapid, survival-level speeds. After I got off the phone with the 911 operator, I rushed into the hallway to tell my neighbors to vacate the building. By the time the New York City Fire Department arrived, my friend and I had already contained the flames, but the fire had done severe damage. The blaze completely destroyed my closet and most of its contents. The wall area and the ceiling surrounding the closet were torched. The firemen told me that if I had been asleep when the fire started, I probably would not have made it out of the apartment alive.

The next morning, as I was cleaning the charred remains of my closet, I salvaged some of my possessions, including my passport and Social Security card. But what was noticeably destroyed and remained only in ashes were the keepsakes from my previous jobs over the years. I used this closet for storage purposes and kept all my papers, training materials, lesson plans, and books from DREAM, Success Academy, and the NYC DOE in boxes. Now those boxes and materials in the closet were utterly ruined. Any physical remnants of the work I accomplished or participated in during my previous roles were gone. So, who was I now?

Since my childhood, I have always chosen to find meaning in even the minor events and coincidences of my life. I was certainly inclined to do the same with a significant event like an apartment fire. While reflecting on the fire, I was reminded of a quote by Heather Ash Amara, a student and teacher of the work of Don Miguel Ruiz, author of *The Four Agreements*, that states, "Allow the fires of transformation to burn away all that doesn't serve you." Considering this quote, I must ask: What elements in my life that no longer served me had this transformative fire burned away? Or maybe a better question is: What disserving elements in my life was the fire attempting to bring to my attention?

As I reflect on those questions, I believe the destruction of the contents in that closet represented a need to destroy the paradigm of our educational system as I knew it, as *we* know it—to burn it down. That is the ultimate reason I have for writing this book. And I further believe that it was no mistake that the fire happened on the same day I discovered I was not offered the full-time role at a traditional educational consulting firm. I was still holding on to a belief that these organizations, though steeped in White supremacy, could truly improve our American educational system for Black and Brown youth. The fire and its destruction were a powerful illustration that I needed to let that mentality go, the mentality that an educational system that had never affirmed and properly taught students of color, could change without having its core intentions and values exposed.

Today my hope is that, like the incident in my apartment, my words will ignite flames of passion. I want my experiences to remind myself and others of the transformative fire burning within us that is necessary to scorch away elements of an American education system that has never served us. May we allow this fire of transformation to empower us to refine our educational system into something new.

———————

TO ACHIEVE THIS transformation and to further understand my experiences in the educational system and those experiences of Black and Brown children like me, I believe it's essential to look at the history of how our American educational system has become an extension of our broader American society. I am a firm believer that understanding our history helps provide context for our present lived experience and is the first step in change. In this vein, let's start with the question: If every system is perfectly designed to get the results it produces, what does that mean for our American educational system?

To help answer that question, we can first look at our American judicial system. As of 2018, incarceration rates are declining in the United States; however, Black Americans are still twice as likely to be imprisoned than their Latino counterparts and five times more likely to be incarcerated than White Americans. These numbers are especially staggering since Black Americans only make up about 13 percent of the overall population in the United States. The historical origins of mass incarceration have been brought to the mainstream by influential thought leaders like Michelle Alexander in her book *The New Jim Crow* (whom I encountered while at Emory University) and most recently Ava DuVernay with her documentary *13th*. These works, along with others, illustrate how the American criminal justice system was *designed* to get the outcome of mass Black incarceration. And I witnessed and experienced the results of this outcome as incarceration has touched numerous Black men in my own family.

Similarly, there is an increasing awareness about the racial wealth and housing disparities within America as more light is shed on redlining practices used by the federal government in the 1930s and continuing to today. These practices have impacted Black wealth by thwarting or deferring homeownership opportunities and still act as a barrier for Black and Brown people, preventing them from living in specific neighborhoods.

However, as Americans grapple with these statistics and their origins, there is still not enough conversation about American educational disparities. As of 2019, the fourth-grade national proficiency rate in reading for Black children is 18 percent compared to 44 percent for White children. These national numbers mirror large states like California, where only 25 percent of Black boys achieve proficiency in reading on the state assessment. Statistics like these outline the incredible racial disparities present in American schools. To comprehend these outcomes, there must be an understanding of the historical context from which America's current public education system emerged.

Many of us were taught that our American public education system was founded on noble ideals by White men such as Horace Mann, John Dewey, and others who believed schools should teach civic virtues and be havens for experiential learning. These ideas and the theory that citizens cannot be "ignorant and free," as Thomas Jefferson put it, were the basis for public, government-controlled education and the common school movement. Though our public education system was built on these idealistic principles, there was an American cancer—a racial caste system—which ultimately permeated the foundation of our public education system as we know it. The cancer of the racial caste system, or White supremacy, was an already mature, malignant tumor present in every element of our society at the time. So even with these ideals of a humanitarian, free public education, Black people were never a true consideration in the conversation. When the idea of mandatory public education started to take root, the ever-present cancer of racism already had a deep hold on the early designs of our public schools.

After slavery ended, Black Americans, ex-enslaved people, could only attend segregated public schools that were severely underfunded and under-resourced. It would not be until the 1954 *Brown v. Board of Education* ruling that schools legally became integrated, though many are still segregated to this day. Additionally, during the Reconstruction era in American history, most White citizens still did not send their children to public schools. School attendance did not become legally mandated nationally until 1918—with Mississippi being the final state to legalize compulsory public education.

As compulsory education spread across the United States and took root, the cancer of racism spread with it. The symptoms of this cancer could be seen in the rhetoric of the initial campaigns, led by national education leaders and elected officials, to "Americanize" all foreign citizens at the dawn of the 1920s, as immigration in America exploded. An influx in immigration led to the fear that "alien ideas and language" would devastate American society. As a result, American education reform efforts were heavily supported by the Ku Klux Klan and other organizations during this time, leading to a national campaign for the expansion of compulsory public education. This charge was grounded in the notion that a population educated in many ideologies should conform to one American philosophy to make a better America—"One people. One America." Further, this eventually led to substantial growth in public schooling and the development of today's massive bureaucratic public education structures.

Understandably, any progressive nation should want to educate its people and create an environment where citizens are literate and acquire necessary skills. This notion was central to Horace Mann's original intention. However, it is the concept of the "Americanization" of all citizens that I believe speaks to a broader issue at hand.

I hope and assume many reading this book would agree that many American values are synonymous with a White supremacist society, placing White people at the top of the societal totem pole. As with various aspects of American life, educational ideals, values, and notions of success have historically been shaped and defined by White men, with little attention to the costs exacted on everyone else.

Therefore, establishing a national public education system that promotes the "Americanization" of its citizens and intentionally excludes Black Americans creates a robust system that functions to devalue non-White citizens and uphold the ideals of White supremacy. Not only were schools segregated by race and class, but the original spread of mandated education had roots in an anti-immigrant, anti-Black movement. Accepting this notion and recognizing the challenges outlined in present-day educational statistics, one can see how our American education system was perfectly designed to produce its outcomes. And perhaps, more importantly, how this design was intentional.

———————

BASED ON DOCUMENTED history, current statistics, and my lived experience in the system, I've concluded that our nation's American public education system is the largest cohesive perpetrator of psychological warfare in this country. Sadly, every child who participates in the system is brainwashed in some way by racial propaganda and false messages about meritocracy that are core to the system's teachings. One definition of psychological warfare is: "things that are done to make someone (such as an enemy or opponent) become less confident or to feel hopeless, afraid, etc." When I think about what has happened to the Black child, or more generally the non-White child, in our public education system since its inception, psychological warfare is the only term that comes to mind. And I would be remiss if I did not acknowledge this psychological warfare is merely an extension of the racialized mental warfare that happens throughout our American society. However, if an educational system is not actively countering the transgressions of its society, then that system is only in place to perpetuate them.

We can see the present-day effects of the psychological warfare that has taken place for over a century. From firsthand experience, I have thirty-two years of familiarity with the impact, and as I have illustrated with my story, this impact has devastating consequences on the development, emotions, and most importantly, the education and life circumstances of millions of children. But let's not just consider my anecdotal accounts; let's look at some statistics.

Aside from the achievement statistics that I mentioned before, the consequences of psychological warfare can most notably be seen in the behaviors of Black children. According to 2017 National Institutes of Health statistics, suicide rates among Black youth (ages ten through nineteen) have increased by 73 percent, while attempts by White youth have decreased over the past thirty years. Sadly, these figures coincide with statistics that Black and Latino adults are much more likely to experience depression than their White counterparts. And I do not want to minimize the costs of psychological warfare only to documented suicide attempts. I would argue that death rates of Black youth are signs of the grave consequences of psychological warfare and the hopelessness that follows. Black youth had the highest rate of gun deaths at the hands of other youth in 2019. More specifically, Black youth are four times more likely to be killed by gun violence than White peers. And even more staggering, Black boys are eighteen times more likely to be killed in gun homicides than White boys. These statistics parallel consistent data highlighting the negative impact public schools have on Black youth—some data indicating that Black youth feel more disconnected in school than their White counterparts.

Further, White teens graduate from high school within four years at rates significantly above Black and Latino teens. With statistics like these, we have barely made incremental strides in addressing the racial disparities facing youth in our schools. And the COVID-19 pandemic has unfortunately exacerbated the already grim disparities. The psychological warfare conducted on our children is real and the consequences are catastrophic, even deadly. So, what do we do now?

———

THE FAILURE OF our traditional model of public education to effectively meet the needs of America's culturally diverse student population has been well documented. Now what is essential is a model and structure that disrupts the mechanism of psychological warfare that causes the long-standing racial and class educational inequities. In thinking about what this model could be, I wanted to examine historical examples of successful culturally responsive, equity-centered, racially affirming educational practices to help inspire solutions for today. The search led me to some of the current work of the Chan Zuckerberg Initiative (CZI).

A report generated between CZI and Raymond Whittaker Design, LLC, outlined three historical educational movements that were the early foundations toward a more liberatory, racially affirming education system to counter the psychological warfare that occurs on Black and other children of color in our traditional public schools. The earliest were the "Freedom Schools" of the 1960s, predominantly in the South and founded by the Student Nonviolent Coordinating Committee (SNCC) in response to the lack of school integration despite the 1954 *Brown v. Board of Education* ruling. In protest to under-resourced, underfunded segregated schools, Black communities, led by the SNCC, decided to start their own. The Freedom Schools taught Black students, and often their parents and grandparents, the social, political, and economic context of race in the United States as well as traditional academic skills. The lessons were inquiry-based and hands-on, and encouraged students to think about their society critically. Over forty Freedom Schools were established across the South. However, they were eventually phased out as public schools became more integrated. We can still find remnants of these schools in the Native American Freedom Schools in Arizona and other similar schools.

The next phase of the liberatory education movement came about in the 1960s and 1970s through the creation of ethnic studies programs in higher education institutions across the country. Ethnic studies evolved out of the civil rights movement as a form of rebellion against the oppressive society that we live in. Now ethnic studies programs cover Black, Asian, Chicano, Mexican, and Native American history and stories. My Race and Ethnic Relations course, probably my most defining course at college, was a product of this movement. The introduction of ethnic studies, in my opinion, has been the most impactful in countering the negative consequences of our public education system. However, ethnic studies at most universities is still voluntary and not a part of the general education requirement established by liberal arts colleges, and are often the first departments to be affected by financial constraints or cutbacks. Therefore, only a self-selecting segment of students are exposed to these courses and teachings.

The CZI and Whittaker report also highlights Detroit as a pioneer in bringing African-centered curriculum to public education in America. The introduction of the African-centered curriculum sprang from the demand from students, parents, and community leaders in Detroit who felt that the public schools were not serving the majority Black student population effectively. After gaining support from the Detroit superintendent, these African-centered schools were free to design their own curriculum and yearly calendar. Like the Freedom Schools, they focused on empowering Black youth through the teaching of Black history and the social, political context of our society. The movement received so much support from the community that the Detroit school board resolved to implement a comprehensive African studies curriculum. However, the comprehensive African-centered school approach phased out because of consistent superintendent turnover, lack of government funding, and shifts in district priorities.

These examples in our history show how Black and Brown people have recognized and rebelled against the miseducation and psychological warfare that occurs in our public education system. However, as evidenced through my own experiences, changing the system is no simple feat—especially a system as comprehensive and widespread as public education. It's a system filled with the mindsets of millions of people, a system that has its own culture or way of life, a system controlled by local, state, and federal governments, a system of rules, regulations, and laws. Therefore, any deviation from the traditional way of doing things would naturally be difficult and filled with fear and uncertainty. The current discussions around critical race theory being taught in schools are prime examples of the fear and uncertainty of change, the perpetual racist backlash against any progress toward true equity. We see on our news stations and in our social media feeds regularly how politicized the conversation has become and the emotional response the conversation has incited in the majority White culture of this country. Shifting mental paradigms is an arduous process and will inevitably cause backlash or pushback. I would argue that the chaos of change is part of what drives the transformation. It is an uncomfortable yet necessary part of the process.

There is hope for our educational future as shown in the historical examples of liberatory education movements. Also, there are present-day examples of districts and schools around the country engaging in this work. The need is ever-present, and the demands of communities are growing. CZI and Whittaker also highlight many schools and a few districts attempting to engage in this work holistically. However, these are only pockets of progress. I still do not believe there has been a systematic approach to move the needle substantially. And the longer we wait, the more children continue to suffer. So, how do we move the needle?

ANY SIGNIFICANT CHANGE in our public education system requires understanding each level of the system and what levers are available for transformative change. As I think about what it means for us to counter the psychological damage our educational system causes, I recognize that any recommendations offered here are only the tip of the iceberg in undoing generations of trauma our education system has inflicted on Black and Brown youth. But I hope that my suggestions will act as a framework for how to navigate this extraordinary task. During the journey of writing this book and hosting a series of talks in preparation for its release, I have been forced to think extensively about how we might do this work. Before I dive into what we might do moving forward, I want to clearly state that I believe the first step is acknowledging the inherent racism embedded within our American educational system. I think this acknowledgment needs to occur at all levels of our society. Our country's leaders, government, school district leaders, principals, teachers, and families all need to acknowledge this truth. We need to admit that though we have been "well-intentioned" in wanting to educate our society, we have perpetuated a social and racial caste system that threatens the very core of our democracy. And I think through this acknowledgment we can then begin to collectively move forward in how we start to right a fundamental wrong.

With that in mind, let's uncover how each level of our educational system can begin to transform itself to create dynamic learning environments where each child can truly thrive.

FEDERAL LEVEL POLICY CHANGE

I watched a recent interview with the current secretary of education, Miguel Cardona, in which he was asked to explain the role of the US Department of Education. He went on to talk about how the federal department of education "pushes for policy changes," and "uses our position to provide grants for things that we know work." More importantly, Cardona explicitly stated that "we do not oversee curriculum... we do not mandate curriculum." This was his way of addressing the controversy that the critical race theory conversation has sparked across the nation. His words were technically true. The majority of educational control and changes happen on the state and local level. Still, he missed a significant portion of context that I think is deeply relevant when we think about the potential of the federal government's role in countering the miseducation that takes place in our American education system.

A shining example was in 1958 when Congress passed the first instance of comprehensive federal education legislation with the

National Defense Education Act (NDEA) in response to the Soviet launch of Sputnik during the Cold War. The passing of this act was intended to help America compete with the Soviet Union in scientific and technical fields and included support for the improvement of science, mathematics, and foreign language instruction in elementary and secondary schools. Under Title III in the NDEA, there was an increase in state education agency "subject matter supervisors" by a whopping 960 percent in just under five years. The responsibility of these subject matter supervisors included curriculum development, in-service education, and Title III project review leading to a drastic enhancement of science and math curricula in schools in each state across the country. In other words, state educational agencies were given the funding and infrastructure support to hire science and math experts to help create and review science and math curricula for schools across their states. The passing of NDEA had significant implications for how science and math were taught in schools across America. As a result, the enrollment in high school science and math classes increased by 50 percent in its first year of implementation. The robust science and math curricula we see now in K–12 education had a basis in this historic act passed in 1958.

I believe if our federal government, led by our federal DOE, created legislation that specifically called for more robust, culturally responsive, racially affirming, social and politically centered curricula in our schools, it would be a way to broadly and systematically impact our educational system as we know it. In the same way that NDEA provided funding for "subject matter experts" to be hired to develop curriculum for schools and infrastructure support to help schools implement the curriculum, our government could take this approach for culturally responsive, racially affirming, empowering educational practices. Legislation such as this would be much more intentional than current standing legislation such as the Every Student Succeeds Act, which focuses on providing additional funding to schools (sometimes referred to as "Title I schools") with students from low-income backgrounds but does not intentionally address those students' psychological and social needs. The passing of NDEA and the Every Student Succeeds Act should teach us that our American government will decisively act to transform our education if they believe it will benefit our country. We need updated federal legislation once again to meet the needs of our students.

In 1958, there was a strong belief that being able to compete in science and mathematics was beneficial to the longevity of our nation. So, my question is, do our leaders genuinely believe that Black and Brown children, along with all other children, being truly empowered in school will be beneficial to the success of our nation? I know my answer—I do.

I also believe others like Secretary for Housing and Urban Development Marcia Fudge do, too. In 2020, she introduced the Black History Is American History Act, which has yet to be approved. The bill would require a more complete teaching of history that includes Black history in all American public schools. If our nation is serious about dealing with the racial crisis in our country and genuinely wants to ensure that every child succeeds, including the Black child, then we need to be intentional, decisive, and bold about the type of legislation we pass and the resources we put behind meeting this challenge.

STATE AND LOCAL LEVEL POLICY AND CURRICULUM CHANGES

As many of us know, most changes to our education system are controlled on the state and local levels. There have been significant inroads in moving toward more culturally responsive education across states and local education agencies. However, there has not been explicit intention on racially affirming and liberatory education. As a result of the uprisings and racial reckoning in the summer of 2020, many states and districts across the country have vowed to add more Black history instruction to their standards. Black history instruction tends to focus on three areas—enslavement of Black people, the Civil War, and the civil rights movement.

And though each of those aspects is important to learn in the context of our American history, I believe that exclusively teaching the history of Black people's oppression within this country only adds to the impact of the psychological warfare that our educational system already causes.

There are many scholars, educators, and even local districts that feel similarly. The School District of Philadelphia was the first district to require an African American course for high school graduation in 2005. And some teachers who are responsible for this instruction have intentionally structured the first semester of the course with empowering students by teaching about the profound history of Africans and the African diaspora before covering the enslavement of African people. Though this is progress, I still believe this is not enough. And, further, limiting empowering teaching about Black people to high school curriculum is a drop in the bucket when it comes to the massive task of countering the lack of empowering education for Black and other marginalized students, especially throughout their most formative years.

I believe that a culturally responsive, racially affirming, liberatory curriculum is critical in elementary school for all students. The instruction should be focused entirely on establishing and supporting a positive racial, cultural, personal identity at the early elementary age. This is a curriculum that empowers all students and emphasizes a powerful self-image. Late elementary and early middle school years are when I believe it would be appropriate to begin exploring the enslavement of African people and the oppressive nature of American society. However, one caveat is that there should be more knowledge and teaching about the enslavement of people that has happened globally—specifically the enslavement of White European people by Black and Arab Moors well into the 1800s. Our schools should give a balanced perspective of our history because we are a nation of people with diverse origins.

States across our union can set standards that require a more thorough racially and culturally empowering curriculum at all levels of a child's K–12 experience. In addition to curriculum changes, states must ensure that the infrastructure, teacher training programs, and resources are available to support educators in teaching holistically, with greater cultural responsiveness. Renowned racial scholar and educator Dr. Gloria Ladson-Billings in an interview with CZI stated, "I think the challenge is the way in which teachers have come to think of their work...so when you ask them to take something like culturally relevant pedagogy that requires the teacher to be the thinker and the decision-maker, a lot of teachers will say, 'We keep hearing about this but nobody's telling us how to do it.' And I'm like, you can't be told how to do it. You have to be able to think your way through it." I believe this statement reflects the type of support teachers need in shifting their mindsets across states and districts to truly implement racially affirming, culturally responsive, liberatory curriculum.

Many districts across the country are engaging in the initial work of countering the White-dominant education that our children receive. And as I have already articulated, there is still much more that needs to be done. But one other area that I believe is imperative in counteracting the psychological impact of our American education system is the restructuring of gifted and talented, or academically tracked, classes as we know them. For many, this notion is controversial and has sparked a national debate, but as I have illustrated in my own story, these tracked opportunities further perpetuate the racial, class, and meritocratic propaganda that I believe is inherent to the psychological warfare schools administer. Now, I want to be clear that I am not saying that I want exceptional educational opportunities to diminish. Still, there must be a much more comprehensive way that all students can access high-quality educational experiences and opportunities in our K–12 system. A recent article published by *The Hechinger Report* examines the national findings that "gifted programs provide little to no academic boost" for students. So, if students truly aren't benefiting from being placed in gifted programs academically but instead are just having access to better opportunities, there is no need to separate students from one another in the way that we do. States and districts must take a critical look at the systems and structures that continue to perpetuate the racial and cultural divide in our schools and find alternative solutions for all students to experience a robust education.

CLASSROOM AND TEACHER–STUDENT INTERPERSONAL RELATIONSHIP CHANGES

For any systemic change to happen in America's public education system, it must be a cohesive undertaking at every level of the system. But it is also clear that the real results felt by students take place at the classroom level and in their interpersonal relationships with their teachers. Studies have shown consistently that teachers have the most significant impact on student achievement, sense of belonging, and overall success. In the education world, this is common knowledge and the basis for continued emphasis on more teacher training and preparation programs. Though more training is beneficial, I want to acknowledge that training is only part of the solution when we think about countering the generational trauma that Black and Brown students arrive at school with, and further experience at the hands of our educational system. And, candidly, often at the hands of "well-meaning" teachers.

As shown in my story, my interactions with my teachers and professors were some of the most memorable interactions that I had within my educational experience. My best and worst memories all came at the hands of my educators. And, I am sure, many people reading this book feel similarly. Therefore, when I think about the classroom changes and the changes that educators can make in countering the psychological warfare in schools, I believe it starts with humanizing the child—especially a child of color. I know my words may seem simple, but we underestimate how often Black and Brown youth are dehumanized in our schools. With an over-focus on test scores, discipline, or our often-unconscious need to "fix" children, we negate the humanity in our students. I feel that truly seeing a child as human, with all the complexities and grace that accompanies that action, can profoundly impact how a child begins to see themself.

As I mentioned before, our public education system is only a reflection of the broader American society, and the consistent dehumanization of Black people is felt throughout all aspects of our society and deeply ingrained in our minds. The mindset that leads to the disproportionate deaths of Black people at the hands of the police is the same mindset that leads to the disproportionate deaths of the aspirations of Black students at the hands of educators.

So, as I take this moment to address teachers, I will do it from my perspective as a Black student and with the context of my shortcomings as an educator. Taking that perspective, what I would have loved from my teachers at every aspect of my educational experience was for them to have humanized me. I would have loved for them to see me as an extension of them, and not separate me, my family, my culture, and my lived experience from theirs. I would have loved for them to tell me that I was worthy, to see me as their child, their nephew, a younger version of who they were, to see me the way that I witnessed teachers often see my White classmates. To see me as "just a good kid." I would have loved for them to give me grace in my unpleasant moments but hold me accountable when I needed to be. To not define me by my worst actions and celebrate my best ones. To attempt to understand me rather than punish me. I would have loved for them to show me their mistakes and to let me know that my mistakes were okay, too. I would have loved for them to ask me about my hopes and dreams and then cultivate them in me. I would have loved for them to have fun with me and show me the joy they felt from being around me. I would have loved for them to work to find what lights me up and empowers me to seek those things that bring me joy. I would have loved for them to center me, not my grades or their curriculum. To value me over my performance. To acknowledge my talents and find ways that I could use them in their classroom. I would have wanted them at every point of the day to let me know that I, and all that I bring, was more than enough.

I firmly believe to begin to counter the racial and social trauma that our children are experiencing daily in and outside of school, educators need to shift our mindset from the traditional approach to fill "empty vessels" (our students) to a mindset of inspiring students to share their innate creativity, insights, and unique talents. This teacher mindset shift I believe builds a positive self-image in students. It encourages students to question the world around them and excites them about learning. It allows students opportunities to see their irreplaceable brilliance and cultivate that brilliance in them. And for many of my White educators reading this book, I would encourage you to release your need to "save" your Black and Brown students and instead set yourself on a mission to give your students the tools, encouragement, and strategies for their own self-actualization. Celebrate every student's greatness and reassure them that their greatness is present even when they do not see it.

These reflections are my wish for educators and students across this country. These words, I hope, resonate with our teachers and enable us to transform the lives of our students.

WHILE RECOUNTING MY time as a teacher at Success Academy earlier in this book, I made it a point to examine my time as an educator with a critical lens. With that, I hoped to illustrate how I played a role in perpetuating the psychological warfare that I outlined in this final chapter. However, as with all teaching and working in service of America's youth, there were also tons of heartfelt and loving moments in my experience. Therefore, as I close out the book, and reflect on what's next in our collective journey, I would like to share a story that I hope can serve as a North Star moving forward.

During my time at Success Academy, as we were nearing the end of the school year, I decided to announce to my class that I would not be coming back the following year due to my admission to the Harvard Graduate School of Education. All the teachers on the third- and fourth-grade teams made bets about how devastated the students would be about the news and how many tears would be shed. But I knew that I could excite my class so they would be happy and not see my leaving as a loss at all. I won those bets, because none of my students cried when I shared the news. They only asked questions like, "How far is Cambridge from Harlem, Mr. Fuller? Can you come visit us every week or can we come visit you?" No tears, only excitement and cheers. There was one student in particular who had become close with me throughout the school year, and though he did not initially show it, I knew he probably was taking the news a little hard. His name was Brandon, and he was a Black boy who was in a traditional public school before joining Success Academy that year.

Brandon joined as a fourth-grade student but was demoted to third grade and put in my classroom because of his "highly aggressive" behaviors. His mother and grandmother removed him from the traditional public school because he often got into fights. They felt that Success Academy would be a safer, more stable environment for him. Though I do believe that Success Academy was a better environment for him, it did not come easy. Brandon had a tumultuous start at our school. He was the cause and initiator of the only physical fight between students in third grade that year, and I had made him apologize to our class for "disrespecting our community." He also pushed me and punched me in the stomach when I stopped him from running out of the classroom when he was enraged and reacting toward another student. Aside from his outburst, he was also very eclectic, liked unique readings and comic books, but did not have the best social skills with other students. Brandon began to settle into the school despite all of his challenges, and I became the "Brandon whisperer." When others could not get through to him, I could. We built a strong relationship throughout the school year. Brandon's response to me was so strong that my principal wanted me to loop with Brandon to fourth grade so I could be his teacher the following year to ensure his overall success at the school.

Consequently, I knew Brandon would likely be upset that I would not be returning. The day after I made my big announcement to the class, Brandon came to me during his free time to chat. This behavior was typical for Brandon as he often liked to talk with me during free moments. However, when he sat on the rug next to my desk, he did not speak at first but instead simply stared at me. I looked at him and asked, "Why are you staring at me, Brandon?"

He responded, "Can you take a picture of me with your cell phone?"

I chuckled a little and thought this was a funny request. I asked him why and he stated, "So you will never forget me." I was touched by his statement and assured him that it was not possible for me to forget him, so he had nothing to worry about. However, in a childlike way he was persistent. And I obliged.

After I took the picture, Brandon stared at me again, smiling, and said, "Mr. Fuller, you're my favorite person in the entire universe."

I looked back at him and said, "Really? Why is that?"

He then looked at me with a seriousness and solemn look on his face. He replied, "Because you're just awesome. And you're the only person who makes me feel good about being me."

I often reflect on Brandon's words and think about the powerful meaning behind them. And his words bring me to one of my favorite quotes by the late Dr. Maya Angelou from one of her talks: "You alone are enough." When I think about her words, I think about how so much of my story as a Black child in our American society and public education system, and now a Black man working in education, has been around this notion of "being enough." From the moment I saw my father behind the glass partition in the jail at the age of three, to witnessing my first-grade classmate Eric being harshly punished, to the pressure I put on myself to be the most well-behaved and most intelligent student in my classes, to my teachers telling me that the Black history I wanted to learn was not important, to feeling that I needed to defend myself against other Black students and later my White teachers and administrators, to the imposter syndrome I felt in my workplace, to the fear I regrettably instilled in Black and Brown children like me—in every stage of my life the question that persisted was "Am I enough?" Whether I was defending that I was enough, trying to convince myself and others that I was enough, or doubting that I was enough altogether, it all came down to the same question.

I believe "Am I enough?" is a question that every human being grapples with at some point in their lifetime, but I think that the Black child grapples with the question often and is given a clear answer by our American society and education system daily. That untrue answer has been clear for generations. Just ask my grandparents, parents, siblings, aunts, uncles, cousins, friends, and millions of Black Americans like them. And as I mentioned in this chapter, the journey between the question and the answer is guided by the psychological warfare experienced within our public schools.

So, as I think about what's next for me, I first hope to embody Angelou's quote "you alone are enough" more intentionally and recognize that as a Black man, my perspective, message, talents, skills, and insights are enough. And then, as Brandon so brilliantly reminded me, our charge is ensuring that every Black and marginalized child in this country feels good about being who they are. Or, more specifically, it's time for us to "get about the business" of transforming our nation's educational system to be a place where Black children, and all children, can leave knowing that they have a place in our society. They can leave knowing that their voice, insights, creativity, talents, and contributions are necessary to the fabric and success of our nation. Black children can leave our public education system, undoubtedly asserting, "I am enough."

Acknowledgments

THE JOURNEY FOR writing this book was harder than I could have ever imagined but it has been one of the most rewarding experiences of my life. I am so thankful that I have been able to create a book that I know will positively impact others. There were many people who have contributed to this process, and I want to take this opportunity to properly thank them.

To my mother: It will be no surprise to you to say you were the first person whom I told the full outline and concept of this book to when it came to me in your living room. Thank you for believing in me and encouraging me every step of the way in this writing process. Thank you for being my rock throughout my life. Because of you, I am. And for that I will forever be grateful.

To my father: Thank you for enduring all that you have endured in life and for illustrating to me the ups and downs of the human experience. Your life, struggles, perseverance, hopes, and dreams have inspired this book and I write this book for your younger self as well as my younger self. I truly thank you.

To my aunts, Damonica and Tajuana, my uncle Mahdi, and my cousin Diamond: Thank you for being early readers of my outlines and book chapters, looking at book cover ideas, and giving me important feedback that helped shape how I told critical stories throughout the book. Thank you for supporting me and encouraging me the entire way through.

To my grandparents and the rest of my family: Thank you for being the foundation that I stand on and giving me the courage to express my opinions to the world. I hope you feel honored by this book and know that your shoulders are what hold me up.

To my dear friend, writing coach, and book champion, Peter Witzig: Thank you for being with me in this process from the very beginning and helping me take my book to the next level. I absolutely could not have done this without you. You have been an angel on earth for me in this writing process and I am forever grateful that you have been by my side in this journey.

To Dale Russakoff: Thank you for being the first "expert opinion" that I spoke to about my book idea and sent my outline to. Your belief in me, feedback, and words of affirmation gave me the initial confidence to continue to pursue the completion of this book for the world to read.

To friends and mentors: Bukie, Brian H., Brandon, Adam, Pam, Marina, Dr. Nadine Sullivan, Nicole, Mukhtar, Sara, Josh, Mac, Sam, Ketica, Allyson, Alain, Greg, Elana, Gabrielle, Donna, Carol Rodgers, and many more, thank you for supporting this process, providing feedback, organizing and attending talks, and just overall checking in on my progress. Your support has been invaluable.

To my influential teachers/professors: Ms. Hilton, Mrs. Watts, Mrs. Ortmann, Mrs. Unsworth, Mr. Johnson, Ms. Lee (Mrs. Shuler), Mr. Taylor, Mrs. Sullivan, Ms. Mulholland, Mrs. Flaherty, Dr. Christine Ristaino, Celeste Lee, and Alisa Berger, thank you for being beacons of light in my educational experience.

To Abdul Tubman: Thank you for writing the foreword to my book, introducing me to my agent, Mark Gottlieb, and supporting me. I appreciate you.

To Mark Gottlieb: Thank you for being my agent and believing in me and my book to pitch to publishers. You have been a needed-behind-the-scenes champion of the book and I am grateful to you.

And last but certainly not least, **to Leticia Gomez and the Kensington Books team**, thank you for being phenomenal partners in the publishing of this book and providing me with the necessary feedback and tools to get the book across the finish line. You have been a pleasure to work with and I am thrilled that this book is being published by Kensington.

With love and gratitude,
Brian Rashad Fuller